Me and My Pet Peeves

Me and My Pet Peeves

Muriel Larson

BROADMAN PRESS
Nashville, Tennessee

Dewey Decimal Classification: 248.4
Subject Headings: CHRISTIAN LIFE

Library of Congress Catalog Number: 87-25646

Unless otherwise stated, all Scripture quotations are from the HOLY BIBLE *New International Version,* copyright © 1978, New York Bible Society. Used by permission. Scripture quotations marked (KJV) are from the King James Version of the Holy Bible. Scripture quotations marked (TLB) are from *The Living Bible.* Copyright © Tyndale House Publishers, Wheaton, Illinois, 1971. Used by permission.

Library of Congress Cataloging-in-Publication Data

Larson, Muriel.
    Me and my pet peeves / Muriel Larson.
        p. cm.
    ISBN 0-8054-5060-2 (pbk.) : $3.25
    1. Christian life—1960-   I. Title.
BV4501.2.L34 1988   87-25646
248.4—dc19   CIP

To my beloved Mother
Helen Fretz Koller
who has always encouraged me
in my ventures
and who has often told me,
"If at first you don't succeed,
try, try again!"
which is good advice for all children,
indispensable for a future writer

Introduction

How do we cope in a Christian way with people who annoy us—such as the gossip, the belittler, the debater, the complainer, the fractious neighbor? And how can we keep ourselves from driving other people crazy?

The principles found in God's Word can not only teach us how to cope with pet-peeve kinds of people but also show us how to stop being a peeve ourselves so reactions can be kept in check. It doesn't always come easy to live by those principles. It usually requires a big hunk of humility, but the end results more than justify the means.

One of the greatest benefits we experience by living with people according to the Bible is the peace and joy we ourselves experience. And if there is anything an irritating person can do, it is to rob us of those precious blessings Christ wants us to have.

Then there are those day-to-day irritations that can cause us chagrin and maybe sleepless nights. How do we handle them so they don't get us down? Again, God's Word comes to our rescue. Of course, God has an answer for everything!

I don't pretend to know all the answers. But during the years I have walked with the Lord, He has taught me some truth through His Word and His Spirit. In this book we'll look at various situations and people that can be like "burrs under the saddle" to us. We'll consider how we can deal with peevish persons and predicaments—and come through with peace.

—*Muriel Larson*

Contents

1.

When Even the Kitchen Sink Breaks Down

It was one of those weeks when I wished Murphy's Law had a neck so I could wring it. You know, that horrible, inexorable force that hits all of us at times: If something can go wrong, it will. When this force strikes us, we start singing "In the Sweet Bye And Bye" for the first time in five years (so maybe it's good for us).

I think it all started when I got twelve rejections in the mail on Monday. As a free-lance writer, I began to suspect then it might be a bad week. As if that weren't rough enough, two rejections came for articles that had been accepted, and one for a book the publishers had considered for a year!

Am I losing my touch? I wondered despondently.

"There goes your career down the drain!" the devil hissed.

One of my back teeth started aching. I stuck my tongue on it. That didn't help. *Oh, no,* I thought, *don't tell me I'm going to have to visit the dentist again!* (Along with several million other people, I hate to go to the dentist!) The ache came and went during the day. So the little question about calling the dentist nagged.

11

That evening when I made my usual visit to my widowed mother, she said, "Don't forget, Muriel, I have an appointment with Dr. Brown tomorrow morning at 10 o'clock."

"Oh, Mom," I clapped my head with my hand, "you know morning is my prime creative writing time! And I had something I really wanted to get out tomorrow. Why didn't you make the appointment in the afternoon like I asked you to?"

Mom gave me her sweet, bland look and answered, "Because that's the time the secretary said to come, and I didn't want to put her to any trouble."

I usually go right to sleep at night. But after a day like this, my mind started dwelling on the various problems, and I tossed and turned. Finally I started talking to God.

"Father," I said, "I know You are in charge of everything. You know all about the rejections and my keen disappointment. But I forgot the prime encouragement for my work: that if something I send out isn't accepted, You may have a more preferred place for it.

"Sure, it's a blow to my ego to receive these particular rejections. But I probably needed that to remind me that You're supposed to take first place in my life—not *me!* So thank You for the assurance that Your hand is on everything that happens in my life—even rejections!"

Next I considered the toothache. *So what's the worst that can happen?* I asked myself.

"You'd have to go to the dentist," came the answer.

"Aren't you glad you have a good dentist to go to? How would you like to live in Ubangiland and have a witch-doctor just yank your teeth out one by one until they're all gone?"

The language wasn't exactly what the Lord might use, but I felt the thought probably came from Him. "You're right, Lord," I said. "Thank You, thank You so much that I live in a land like this where I can keep my own teeth!"

As I lay there praising and thanking the Lord for this blessing, the ache subsided, and suddenly I didn't mind if I did have to go to the dentist.

Then I thought about Mom and her appointment. "Lord," I said, "Mom is so dear to me. I am thankful to You that I still have her and can still do for her. Maybe that appointment was made in the morning so I'd finally have the time to revise those articles sitting on my desk!"

So peace came into my heart about that matter, too. I turned over and let my mind rest. The next thing I knew, it was morning.

Nothing else disturbing happened until Wednesday. That's when I got the call from my daughter's school. "Mrs. Larson, Lori has had an accident," the secretary reported.

"Is she all right?" I gasped.

"Well, she's all right," answered the secretary, "but I really can't say the same for your car."

A neighbor drove me to the school. After he let me out, I headed for the police car parked nearby. The officer was writing out tickets for my daughter and the other driver.

Then Lori went into the school, and I checked out my car. Rammed into the right front side, it looked like a three-dimensional model from a Salvador Dali painting. When I started the car, something clattered as if it had a mortal wound. And I couldn't move the gearshift.

I prayed while a mechanically-gifted teacher looked my car over. "You need a new fan," he advised. "But the chassis has been knocked out of place, and I'm afraid this is a total."

"What am I going to do without a car, Lord?" I wondered, my heart sinking. I began praying hard.

Miraculously, the teacher manually put the car into

"drive"; we took it to a body shop, where the chassis was put back into place for $5! I had a used fan installed at a junk yard for $7. And my car worked!

That afternoon when I drove over to pick up Lori from school, I thought, *Oh, praise the Lord that I can actually use my car to pick Lori up—and that she isn't in the hospital now instead of school!* So even though my car looked a mess, God gave me something to rejoice about. A month later He gave me a car in much better condition—and newer.

On Friday I discovered that the kitchen sink was leaking. I pulled everything out, put a pan under the leak, and cleaned up the mess. Then looking at that dripping pipe, I thought, *That's just like the burrs under our saddle that seem to stick us one by one—the steady drip!*

"Father," I said then, looking up, "if You and I hadn't taken care of that other junk this week, I think I'd be a basket case by now! And oh, is there anything I can do to stop this leak myself?"

I examined the leak closer. It came from a flange. *Maybe all it needs is tightening!* Borrowing a large wrench from a neighbor, I tightened the flange—and the leak stopped. *Wow,* I thought, *how simple!* Yet how much concern such a thing could cause and how much money it might have cost to be fixed! So I thanked the Lord for His help.

And the toothache? After that first night the ache never returned. And that's like many of the seeming irritations we encounter in life. They're really not worth worrying about or losing sleep over. Mark Twain said, "I am an old man and have known many troubles, but most of them never happened!"

Why should we let the petty irritations of life get us down when the Lord can pick us up? He advises us in Philippians 4:4-7, "Rejoice in the Lord always. . . . Do not be anxious about anything, but in everything, by prayer and petition, with thanksgiving, present your requests to God. And the peace of God, which transcends all understanding, will guard your hearts and your minds in Christ Jesus.''

2.
Patience Is a Virtue — but Who Wants to Wait?

Did you ever go into a discount store and have a few items to buy and only seven minutes left on your lunch hour?

You look over the checkout lanes and spot what seems to be the shortest line. The clerk has just taken care of one person, and two others are waiting. One has two items and the other, three. *Ah,* you breathe hopefully, *that should just take a couple of minutes.* So much for famous last thoughts!

The woman with two items waits for the clerk to ring them up—and *then* slowly takes out her checkbook. She fishes around in her purse and finally finds a pen. Then she carefully, in Palmer-rolling penmanship, writes the check for $1.59. "Uh, who do I make it out to?" she drawls at the clerk.

She finally hands the check to the clerk, who rings a bell and waves the check. Three minutes later a woman comes to OK the check. The clerk gives change, and the woman fools around in the lane for another minute trying to put her checkbook and pen back into her purse.

By this time you have a case of Saint Vitus' dance.

The man behind her steps up and lays down his three

purchases. *Ah,* you breathe a sigh of relief, *men don't usually pay for just a few items with a check.*

Two items require price checks, and clerks are called to verify from the farthest corners of the store (located in Lower Slobbovia). They finally come and then go back to their country to check. After five minutes the prices are verified. *Then* the man gives his charge card to the clerk.

You look up mournfully and silently say, "Lord, why wasn't I born a hundred years ago when life was more leisurely and there were no such things as checks, charge cards, and price checks?"

I have one encouraging word about this frantic age we live in: This is no doubt the "time of the end" that the angel from God told Daniel about. The angel predicted of this age, "Many shall run to and fro, and knowledge shall be increased" (Dan. 12:4, KJV).

So, while you're standing in line, it's a great time to get right with the Lord. For according to the Bible, Jesus may come at any time during the "time of the end!"

You see—there's always something to be thankful for.

Standing in line to get your driver's license or license plates can require a lot of patience. One day when I went to the Motor Bureau, there were three lines that ran almost back to the entrance. And the clerk tending my line went out for a coffee break or some other twenty-minute safari.

I stood in back of a bearded guy who wore blue jeans and a T-shirt that said, "Your place or mine?"

But he was more interested in talking to the cute blond woman in front of him than passing the time of day with a woman old enough to be his mother. That's OK though—he wasn't my type.

I found someone far more my type to talk to—someone caring, with great power, someone who could make my dreams come true.

"Hey, how can I meet someone like that?" I can hear a reader asking.

Look up. He's just a prayer away!

Sure—waiting in line, in a doctor's or dentist's office, in a traffic jam, or on the phone provides some tremendous opportunities to talk to the Lord.

What shall we talk about? Well, everyone has problems. Now's the time to get into an in-depth discussion with the Lord about them. If you're His child, He is interested in every detail of your life. I have often found that while I'm discussing some problem of my own or someone else's that my mind is tuned with the Lord's; for at such times He puts answers and ideas in my mind that work out beautifully.

All around us—in church, neighborhood, and business— are people with problems. God wants us particularly to care about our fellow Christians. Do you hear the latest news? The Smiths have broken up; the Joneses got offended and have dropped out of church; the Browns' son has been into drugs and has gotten in trouble with the law; three people you know of are in the hospital. You can make a difference by interceding for God's helping hand in these troubled lives.

As a counselor for a Christian television program I probably hear more sad burdens than most people do. Our Christian brothers and sisters are hurting. Do we really care? One of the best ways we can help them is through prayer. For our Father owns the cattle on a thousand hills. He knows where every good job is. He still heals and saves souls when Christians pray.

While we're waiting, whether it is for three minutes or an hour, we can make the time fly by not only praying for the needs of others around us, but also praying for missionaries, by name, around the world. They need prayer for grace, encouragement, various needs, wisdom, their children, their work, their converts, their protection.

When was the last time you prayed for your pastor, the church staff, the leaders, the teachers, and workers in your church? If we regularly pray, "Lead us not into temptation, but deliver us from the evil one" (Matt. 6:13) not only for ourselves and our church leaders, but for all Christians, how many might be kept from falling into sin and bringing shame on Christ's name and sorrow into their own lives and those of their loved ones?

One of the instructions given to Christians in Ephesians 6 for spiritual warfare and protection is this: "And pray in the Spirit on all occasions with all kinds of prayers and requests. With this in mind, be alert and always keep on praying for all the saints" (v. 18).

Would the Spirit be present in mightier power in our churches if we prayed for our leaders and fellow Christians every time we had to wait? Would our country, or our world, be in better shape if we prayed for its leaders, as the Bible tells us to?

And would we be in better shape spiritually if we spent all that waiting time talking to our Lord? There's no doubt about it, is there? Paul told us to "pray without ceasing"— not hard to do while waiting in a dentist's office, in preference to thinking about the forthcoming drill!

I have also found that waiting in offices and lines sometimes provides me with good opportunities to talk to others about the Lord. The hurting people all around us don't merely need to be prayed for—they need to hear about the Person who can change their lives. Or, if they are Christians, they may need encouragement to live for the Lord and look to Him.

I've found an approach to ensure that the Lord will give me someone to speak to for Him. The first thing I do when I awake each morning is to report for duty. I say, "Here I am, Lord—if there is anyone You want to reach or help, use me!" And he does.

So, we can stew and fret when we have to wait, and get ourselves in an abominable state. Or we can make the best of the situation, and, as Paul said to the Ephesians, make the most of every opportunity we have for doing good (5:17). His suggestions for how to do this parallel and add to those already given. These are found in verses 18-20.

"Try to find out and do whatever the Lord wants you to. . . . Be filled instead with the Holy Spirit and controlled by him. Talk with others about the Lord, . . . making music in your hearts to the Lord. Always give thanks for everything to our God and Father in the name of our Lord Jesus Christ" (TLB).

3.

The Bad News Blues

I had just arrived home after speaking to a mother-daughter banquet when the phone rang. It was my sister-in-law calling from Florida. "Gene died at six o'clock this evening," she sobbed.

I was so stunned I couldn't say a word at first. My beloved brother, my only brother, my big, handsome brother dead? Finally I stammered, "I know he's been ill for quite some time, Betty—but I didn't realize he was so close to dying!"

Betty told me what had happened that week. Even though he was ill, Gene had kept on working in his position as drug abuse counselor at Tyndale Air Force Base because if he died he wanted his wife and children to be provided for. A coworker had brought him home that Monday, and Gene had collapsed on the front door step.

My heart was so heavy as I learned of my brother's last days. "Oh, why did my brother have to die in the prime of life, Lord?" I cried. "It's not fair! I have no sister, and Gene was my only brother, and we were so close. And now he's gone!"

As I hung up the phone, I wondered how I would tell my

elderly mother. My father had died only two years before, now this! I felt overwhelmed.

"Oh, Lord, help!" I cried silently. And He did. From that moment on I felt as if I were supported in a cloud. The Lord helped me tell my mother and comfort her. As we drove to Florida, as we attended the funeral, as we drove home, I still felt as if I were on a plane of grace that was indescribable. The Lord delivered me from my peevish spirit. I no longer questioned Him.

I have grieved for my brother, though, and for my father before that. But how comforting it is to know that someday I shall see them again in heaven. That is the Christian's blessed hope.

A number of people I have known, however, have been so crushed by bad news that the fretting, grieving, or self-recrimination has affected their lives for weeks, months, or years. I do believe my brother's physical problems began when a business venture of his failed, and he took it very hard. Some time after that he developed colitis, which ultimately led to his needing a colostomy—which I believe eventually played a part in his death.

We are only human. It is only natural for us to be affected adversely by bad news. But it is dwelling on it that deeply hurts us.

Peter's advice to Christians, by inspiration of the Holy Spirit, is still good today: "Cast all your anxiety on him because he cares for you" (1 Pet. 5:7).

In this life we all get hit with bad news from time to time. Some is harder to take than others; but bad news, especially when it comes in bunches, can certainly trouble us like burrs under the saddle, can't it?

Bad news almost always comes about like this:

Monday: "I'm sorry, Buddy, but you need a new transmission."

Tuesday: "Your brakes are shot, too."

Wednesday: "I got laid off for two weeks, Honey."

Thursday: "Shawn got into a fight at school today, and a front tooth was knocked out."

Friday: "Michelle got bit by a dog. She may need rabies shots."

Saturday: "Mother's coming to visit."

Sunday: "Lord, where are You? Help!"

We all have weeks like this, especially my next-door neighbor. I've made a career out of helping her through such times. And through this opportunity I have been able to influence her to a closer walk with the Lord. I have seen her learn to trust the Lord more and more.

James 1:2-5 says, "Consider it pure joy, my brothers, whenever you face trials of many kinds, because you know that the testing of your faith develops perseverance. Perseverance must finish its work so that you may be mature and complete, not lacking anything. If any of you lacks wisdom, he should ask God, who gives generously to all without finding fault, and it will be given to him."

When we who are Christians encounter life's trials, we can know that these things will increase our faith and patience if we allow them to. If we kick against the pricks—get peevish, rebel, resent, become bitter, carry the load ourselves—we'll stay spiritual babes and fail to grow to the place where we can meet each trial with serene faith in the Lord.

So when we are deluged with bad news, let's take it all to the Lord, ask Him for wisdom to know what to do about it, and leave it with Him. As we realize His guidance and sustaining grace, we'll feel so much better about everything.

4.

Things That Self-destruct

What do we do when the top flies off the saltshaker, half the ketchup bolts out on our liver, our camera flash conks out when we want to take a shot of Aunt Gussie, whom we haven't seen for twenty years, or we have a flat tire 200 miles from home—and discover our spare is shot? (That happened to me!)

Well, sometimes we make like Mount Vesuvius and practically self-destruct ourselves (fuming, high blood pressure and all that). When we do that at the dinner table, it destroys all that sweet peace and calm we were having up to that point. Er, this applies to about 13 percent of family dinner tables anyway.

"Who didn't screw this saltshaker top back on right?" we scream.

Then our mate replies testily, "You know who filled the saltshaker last!" (If it was us, we suddenly stop spewing lava and remain silent for the rest of the meal.)

The picky person simply keeps quiet about the matter, picks the food-laden plate up, and tosses the salt-encrusted meal in the garbage, along with the offending saltshaker. The less-picky person who prepared the food then proceeds to make like Mount Etna. The picky person leaves for the nearest fast-food place.

Cameras, especially their flash attachments, have a nasty tendency to self-destruct at exactly the wrong time. Even worse than failing to get a photo of a favorite aunt have been my experiences in this area. When I interview people to write their personal experiences or articles about their work, I usually take photographs of them.

Now the flash attachment or camera has never self-destructed when the interview takes place at my home or a mile away from where I live. No, the crafty thing waits until I interview somebody who lives in Outer Mongolia, on a gray, rainy day, yet—and *then* it conks out!

You know what I mean in a situation like this. Here I am, supposed to be this good Christian person, interviewing this other good Christian person. And I have to keep my cool while I'm screaming inside, *Yikes, what do I do about getting photos now!*

Another one of the vital pieces of equipment in my work has been my typewriter, which has a number of things that can self-destruct just as I've been typing the last page of a manuscript that I wanted to mail out that day.

One day the ornery thing made a fatal mistake. It sttarttted sttutttering while I was working on an assignment with a deadline.

"OK, machine, I've had it!" I exclaimed indignantly. "I'm going to buy a word processor!"

So now I have a word processor, and I really love it! It only has this one little problem

Oops! The power just went off for two seconds, and I lost two pages of some really hilarious stuff. Sorry about that!

And hey, all you gardeners out there! Have you ever pulled obstinate weeds with roots that go halfway to China (like Bermuda grass) and had your elbow self-destruct? I have. So you go around telling people about your strange painful elbow, and some bright person exclaims, "Oh, you have tennis elbow! You need an A-bandage for that!"

"Tennis elbow?" you ask in wonder. "How can I have tennis elbow when I haven't played tennis for ten years?"

Trust me—I think in view of the fact that more gardeners probably acquire "tennis elbow," we ought to campaign to have it called "gardeners' elbow."

For a while I kept my A-bandage on active duty, until I realized I was not only hurting my body—I was hurting the temple of God! Now instead of using "pull power," I use "dig power."

You know, when things self-destruct by themselves, there may not be much we can do. But I think that when we contribute to the self-destruct—especially when it's God's temple we're doing it to—then with God's help we ought to cut it out.

If we don't stop contributing to the self-destruct, let's not complain when we can't garden much any more, or when the doctor says, "You've got to give up all sugar, salt, and fat stuff!"

Aren't you glad we have the unlimited power of God to draw on to help us overcome dumb ways of living? I am!

Nobody has to tell us what self-destructs the worst. We all know it's our vehicle of transportation, which I believe has approximately 357,233 parts that may self-destruct at any one of 218 wrong times. Of course, I may be prejudiced in this area. My car is a vintage 1974 model that has really given me a fun time (while training me in patience).

My latest adventure was a recent Sunday morning when I was dressed to the top of my head, all ready to go in to church and practice and play the organ for the morning service. The car started, I drove down the street to pick up my mother, pulled in her driveway—and the car stalled. It wouldn't start again. And nothing that her neighbor or I could do would make it start. He hooked his charger up to the battery. But when it was 10:30 we discovered it wasn't the battery—it was the starter.

Have you ever noticed that it's not the thing you can fix that breaks down at a time like that—it's something you need a wrecker for to take your car to the garage?

The neighbor obligingly drove us to our church across town. My hair was a mess (from riding on my bicycle when coming back from my house with something), and I had lost my favorite blue net cap. But I made church barely in time to turn on the organ, set up my music, and play the prelude!

Years ago something like this might have come close to giving me a nervous breakdown. But I've had a lot of experience with things that self-destruct; and through these experiences the Lord has taught me how to deal with them, so I can ride over them instead of under them.

I think the Scripture that has helped me the most in this area is Proverbs 3:5-6: "Trust in the Lord with all thine heart; and lean not unto thine own understanding. In all thy ways acknowledge him and he shall direct thy paths" (KJV).

How does that help? Well, it gives me the serenity of knowing that no matter what happens I can lean on my Lord. No matter what happens, I know He'll work things out. I know He wants me to have His peace and joy at all times and doesn't want me to fret about such little matters as things that self-destruct. Nothing is important enough for us to self-destruct ourselves by exploding, getting mad at God or man, or fretting about all the problems we may face when something goes ker-flooey.

I've learned that the best way for me to cope is to praise the Lord for things I can be thankful for. In the matter of photographs, I have thanked the Lord that the persons I have interviewed have supplied me with better shots than I could have taken.

In the matter of my car not starting that Sunday morning, listen to all the things I found to be thankful for!

Usually my mother awaits my coming by the side of the road. But this time she didn't—so my car stalled in her driveway.

By refusing to start in her driveway instead of mine, I had the help of Mother's next-door neighbor, a retired mechanic. Then he offered to drive us to church, and we arrived there in time. I praised God for these things and refused to think about the incapacitated car.

One family in our church lived on our side of town, and they brought us home. The next day my repairman sent a wrecker to pick up my car. There was $25 on the top of the bill—but it had to be done.

My pastor called and told me he had felt impressed to take up a special offering for me during the Sunday evening service. "We all appreciate you, Muriel," he explained. (Hearing that almost made the car breakdown worthwhile!) The offering came to $96. So did the car repair bill!

Such experiences as this can prove to be truly heartlifting, just to have the thrill of seeing how our Father works matters out when things self-destruct!

5.
When People Don't Listen

Did you ever start talking to someone and wonder if that person was really listening to you? You drop a question and get a blank stare. You're not particularly happy about this reaction. It implies that you've been Boresville as far as that person is concerned, doesn't it!

I have this problem with my Mom at times. I'll be talking away, then suddenly she'll say, "Oh, did I tell you what Marie said to me the other day?" Sometimes I think she does this to keep her blood pressure from going up. I'll have to watch what I say, too!

Now this isn't too bad between a mother and daughter, at least not in our case, because I am always praying the Lord will help me have patience with my mother because of her age. And He's giving me all these opportunities to practice it!

But this business of not really listening to someone is terrible when it happens with a husband and a wife. A man will come home from work eager to share with his wife what a rough day he had. He needs somebody to complain to, and sometimes what does he get? After three sentences his wife asks him, "Honey, did you remember to stop at the supermarket and pick up some bread?"

Now there may be "honey" on that, but what the poor guy hears loud and clear is a voice in his mind that says, *She's just not interested in what happens to me. She doesn't care if I live or die!*

A wife may encounter the same problems with her husband. Here she is stuck at home with four hyperactive children under the age of seven. Naturally she can't wait until her husband comes home to share with him the misdeeds, mishaps, and downright disasters of the day.

Twenty seconds into the account he asks blandly, "Is supper ready? Guess I'll go watch the news on TV." Then he saunters out to the den. She stands there with her hands on her hips, glaring at his retreating back. If looks could kill, he'd be lying flat on the floor!

And then, of course, there are the teenagers. Have you ever tried to get through to your teenager who has a plug in his ear and a nose in a comic book? Might as well try to communicate with a deaf Ubangi!

I've often had this problem with my younger daughter, and it has driven me up the wall at times. For some reason the only time she really listens and hears me is when she comes wailing to me with problems. This is an excellent time to talk to your kid, because then the hearing ability is excellent and attention beam on full. I've also found it helpful to go for walks with Lori, for then, too, we can communicate.

I suspect that usually teenagers don't want to listen to their parents because they don't like what they hear—it's usually a lecture or an admonition of some sort such as, "Go straighten up your room and make your bed." Such remarks don't win popularity contests with teenagers who prefer to ignore such mundane things.

So how do we reach them when it's necessary to communicate? We gently pull the ear plug or cut off the TV, face them squarely, and command, "Read my lips!" Then we deliver our soliloquy in brief form. If it's something we want them to do, we gently take them by the arm, help them up, and head them in the right direction. I'm not claiming this will always work—but it sure beats talking to yourself!

I think we are all probably guilty of not listening to someone at one time or another. So, none of us can throw stones. Let's put ourselves in the other person's place. If we do that, we will become more considerate of others.

I think it's most important for us to pay our family members the respect of listening to them. If we show such respect to our mates and children, then we set an example for them to reciprocate. Where else can we feel so free to pour our hearts out?

A husband and wife should have the closest relationship of any two people in this world. We may often patiently listen to others pour out their troubles to us—but impatiently cut off that closest person to us, the one who needs us most. I wonder how many marriages would be saved if husbands and wives would regularly sit down and talk with each other and really listen! Why should they have to go to a marriage counselor to do that?

Christianity elevated women, and wherever we find true Christianity, women live in much better conditions than most of those who live in pagan cultures. We discover even in nature, however, that there must be a chain of command. So in God's Word we find it, too. God is at the top; rulers and all those in authority are to be obeyed; the husband is the head of the wife; children are to obey their parents. When this rule is followed in love, then there is order and peace.

The apostle Peter wrote to wives that they were to be in

subjection to their husbands, as Sarah was to her husband Abraham, calling him lord (1 Pet. 3:1-6). If a woman looks up to her husband as the leader of her home and heart, then she will listen to him when he speaks; then she will cooperate with his wishes whenever possible, and it won't be burdensome.

Peter also told the husbands to give honor to their wives (1 Pet. 3:7). The Greek word used here, *time,* means "valuing." If a man values his wife, gives her honor, will that not affect her reaction and love for him? If he values her, he will value her opinions; he will also give her the respect of listening to her. Many people who go to psychiatrists might not need to if they only had a loved one who would listen!

Peter indicated that if husbands and wives do not give honor to one another, their prayers are hindered. No wonder so many marriages fall apart! They are victims of neglect, of uncaring partners, of lack of respect, of unanswered prayer.

Lack of interest in listening breeds a spirit of resentment, bitterness, rebellion. These attitudes not only stand between us and others, but between us and God. So if a person won't listen to us, let's not let it make us bitter or resentful, because we only hurt ourselves physically, emotionally, and spiritually. Let's reject such attitudes. Let's try to persuade the other person to talk with us—but if he or she won't, then let's forgive the heedless person and take it to the Lord. He's always willing to listen!

6.

Worries and Fears

Worries and fears are exceedingly annoying, and they afflict all of us. They keep us awake at night, tossing and turning, the nasty little mind-tormenters that make us peevish. Most are unnecessary.

In his book, *Release from Tension,* Dr. Paul E. Adolph wrote, "Anxiety and worry represent forms of fear which project themselves into the future and often concern themselves with imaginary situations which never come to pass. Indeed, it often happens when the future situation arrives, it is devoid of all the contemplated elements which are anticipated."

Mark Twain said, "I am an old man and have known many troubles, but most of them never happened." Psychologists say that 90 percent of the things people worry about never come to pass.

Shortly after a friend of mine moved from Massachusetts to South Carolina, she became acquainted with some neighborhood children. One day a boy told her something that made her hair stand on end. "The people who lived here before had a dog," he said, "and the dog had puppies. But the wolf rats killed them!"

"What are 'wolf rats' ?" Jane asked.

"Great big rats!" he exclaimed. "They come from the water, and they live in the woods, and they go into your cellar over there."

As she went into her house, Jane imagined an animal three feet high, six feet long, with teeth like a wolf, and a pointy nose embellished with menacing whiskers—and she was scared to death. She started praying fervently.

When her husband came home, she told him about the "wolf rats," and he just laughed. But, as the days went by, Jane lived in mortal fear of those creatures.

One night after she and Richard went to bed, she heard a noise in the wall. "It's a wolf rat!" she cried, leaping out of bed.

Richard got up groggily and put on his robe. "Here, you'll need a club!" Jane cried, handing him a big stick. Then she ran into her daughter's room to protect her.

So, at 3:30 in the morning, Richard suddenly awoke to find himself standing in the middle of the room with a club. "Why am I doing this?" he asked himself.

While Richard banged on the walls to get rid of the "wolf rats," Jane fearfully cried to the Lord for protection. Finally, Richard persuaded her to come back to bed.

One day the neighbor children were talking about "wolf rats" again. As Jane listened to her children, with their distinct Massachusetts accent and the children with their Southern drawl, something dawned on her. "Would you spell that word *wolf* for me, Billy Joe?" she asked.

"Sure," he exclaimed. "W-A-R-F!"

Jane's face turned red. She knew that was nothing more than a common six-inch dock rat, of which she had never been that scared. The fear had all been in her mind.

When her husband came home she told him the story. He rolled on the floor with laughter.

And Jane went to the Lord and apologized abjectly for not having trusted Him more.

Years ago, when I was a fairly new Christian, I worried about things. One day as I drove to work, I was wondering how we were going to pay our bills. My husband was out of work, and our only income was from the office job I'd found.

I came to an intersection and stopped. Glancing up and down the street, I pulled out. Suddenly I heard screeching brakes and a sickening crunch. I had collided with a car that seemed to come out of nowhere.

I received a repair bill from the driver of the other car a few days later. There was no way we could pay it. Eventually we were sued.

Although I had prayed about our financial situation many times, I didn't yet know about the secret of committing my burdens to the Lord. So I worried.

That next Sunday our pastor quoted Philippians 4:7 for the benediction: "And the peace of God, which passeth all understanding, shall keep your hearts and minds through Christ Jesus" (KJV).

Those words really hit me. *I'm sure not experiencing that peace,* I thought.

When I got home, I opened my Bible and turned to the fourth chapter of Philippians. Verse 6 held the key to my worries: "Be careful for nothing; but in everything by prayer and supplication with thanksgiving let your requests be made known unto God."

I examined each part of that verse. I was not to be anxious about anything. I was to bring everything to the Lord in a spirit of supplication and thanksgiving.

I fell to my knees and followed that verse. Pouring out

my heart to the Lord, I brought to Him every problem. I thanked Him for all He had done in the past and what He would do in the future. Then I knew I could trust Him completely with the whole burden!

Deep-down relief came to me as I left it all with my Lord. Faith moved into my heart to banish all my fears and worries. I knew God was going to help me.

While I was still on my knees a thought came to me. *Why don't you call the man you hit and explain your situation? He might settle for a lesser sum.*

What sweet peace I felt as I stood up. It was truly the peace "which passeth all understanding."

I called the man. When he heard about our situation, he agreed to cancel the suit and settle for twenty dollars. The Lord quickly removed one burden, and He soon removed the rest.

That was many years ago. Through every trouble and emergency since, I've learned that God's formula for peace in Philippians 4:6-7 really works.

7.

Discrimination

Discrimination is a pet peeve of many people, and many of us fall into some group that is discriminated against. No one likes to be belittled or to feel less well-treated than somebody else! I speak as one of you, because I've been there!

There are innumerable people who are paid less than others for doing the same kind of work and perhaps have the same ability. I worked in several places where this was true. In this crowd are those who deserved promotion, but someone less qualified received it. Women and members of minority groups particularly suffer from this type of discrimination—although an effort has been made in recent years to correct this situation.

There are those who have been barred from clubs, hotels, restaurants, residential neighborhoods, churches, schools, or organizations because of their sex or race; and those who have actually been persecuted for the same reason. These often include blacks, Jews, American Indians, and women.

Abraham Rones, a Jewish man who received Christ as his Messiah at the age of thirty-nine, told me how when he was a child, other children whom he thought were Christians would chase him home, throwing stones, and shouting, "Sheeny, Christ-killer, dirty Jews!" It made him sour on all who professed to be Christians.

I know Christians who have suffered discrimination because of their faith. One acquaintance of mine and her husband wanted to open their home to foster children. A social worker came to the home to check on it.

She noticed on Nancy's living room wall a picture of Jesus standing and knocking at the United Nations Building.

"Do you see Jesus as big as that?" she asked suspiciously.

"No, ma'am," Nancy answered. "I see Him bigger than that!"

"Well," replied the woman icily, "we would rather give the children to an atheist than to Christians!"

At first it rankled Nancy that an atheist would be preferred to Christians for the care of children. But as she thought about the situation, she recalled that the Scripture says that those who do not know Christ are blind and under the control of Satan (2 Cor. 4:4; Eph. 2:2). When we realize what God's Word says, and that He has the ultimate authority, we can rest in that.

The Curtises took the matter to the Lord in prayer, because they knew He wanted them to take disturbed, homeless children into their home. Since they had an excellent recommendation as foster parents from another state, they received approval in spite of the social worker's disapproval. They quickly received a houseful of children. Most of the children they have taken in have come to Christ through Nancy or the church the Curtises take them to—and their lives have been transformed. Through Nancy's firm discipline, also, they have been trained to a right way of living far different from their pasts.

I have also encountered discrimination because of my stand for Christ. But Jesus said that if He received such treatment, we who follow Him should expect it as well. Peter said we should rejoice in it. I believe, however, that we should be "as wise as serpents and as harmless as doves," as Jesus instructed.

As Christians who are told by our Master to love our neighbor as ourselves, we should never deliberately antagonize people and goad them into persecuting us. God calls us to peace, and He can give us wisdom in how to do everything He wants us to do. But some discrimination, or even persecution, may be unavoidable if we seek to do God's will. If it comes, rejoice—don't fret!

I have experienced a type of discrimination that many women have undergone—and it certainly has peeved me! For years my husband and I had done business with several nationwide stores. Our charge cards were all in my husband's name, but I always saw to it that the bills were paid on time.

Then came the time when I had to put the charge cards in my name. But I was making my living as a free-lance writer with no set income and living in a rental home. The largest catalog-department store complex turned me down —even though I told them I had paid their bills on time for twenty years! I was stunned.

Not long after that I needed a new washer. I had just received a royalty check, so I could pay for it. But I was allowed to buy it on time from this company. I figured that when they saw how I paid it off in a month or so, they would give me a charge card.

No way! I was refused again.

About this time I was also refused a credit card account by the bank I had done business with for three years, and in which I had a nice savings account.

Again I was ticked off. But by this time in my life I had learned that my Lord didn't want me to be ticked off, because it was bad for my spiritual, emotional, and physical health. So I held this matter up to the Lord. He knows all the answers—right?

He brought to my mind the "Prayer of Serenity" used by the Alcoholics Anonymous group: "God, grant me the serenity to accept the things I cannot change, courage to change the things I can, and the wisdom to know the difference."

The only time I have ever had courage was when the Holy Spirit gave me the power to witness. Otherwise I was a pussycat—I had no nerve. I seldom stood up for myself.

But now I knew I was to quit fretting and do something about this situation. Praying for God's enablement, I went in to the bank and spoke to the manager, pointing out to him the good record I had with the bank (no bounced checks!), as well as the good balance in my checking and savings accounts. In the face of my evidence and persistence, the manager finally caved in and let me have a charge card.

Fortified by this experience I went to see the manager at the department store and laid before him my case (along with letters of recommendation sent by the company to us in times past). He was fascinated by the fact that I was a writer and asked me questions about my work. Before long I had his promise that my charge card would be in the mail.

So I learned that if you can do something about a situation in which you are discriminated against, do it in God's strength and in a pleasant, determined manner. While not everyone we may have to deal with is a Christian, the principle of what Jesus taught about going to your brother if he has offended you may work with non-Christians, too. For there is nothing like talking things out with another person reasonably to help set matters straight and perhaps overcome some type of discrimination.

As Christians we should never be guilty of discrimination toward others! James saw how the early Christians discriminated against the poor among them and gave special preference to the rich. I'm afraid this is still true in many churches today! Do we not often prefer well-to-do deacons to poor ones? Do we not give more respect to those who have money and high positions than to those who are not well off?

Do we not speak disparagingly about people of other races? Do we not bar them from our fellowship? And if another Christian believes differently from us on some minor point of doctrine, might we not look down on that person?

Our Lord Jesus Christ said, "By this shall all men know that ye are my disciples, if ye have love one to another" (John 13:35, KJV).

Romans 13:10 says, "Love does no harm to its neighbor."

8.

Frustrations

Have you ever been running late on Sunday morning—and put on the wrong clothing? If you're a man, you might look down and suddenly realize your socks don't match—and go searching frantically for the other pair of black and blue. If you're a woman, you've jumped into a dress and started zipping it up, and the zipper gets stuck—or, worse yet, caught in your slip.

And then the kids! Michelle walks in and she has quickly grown three inches, and there she is in a dress that hasn't lengthened accordingly while it was laid away for the winter. "Change it now!" you exclaim.

For a change Chad got dressed in his Sunday best with no nagging. He goes outside for two minutes and then returns looking like a refugee from an earthquake.

You all finally pile out of the house, locking the door securely—then dear old Dad discovers he left his keys on the dresser. And dear old Mom suddenly remembers she left her keys in her other purse.

Frustrations! Life is full of them, isn't it! You go on a picnic—and rain comes pouring out of nowhere, along with heavenly fireworks and appropriate booms. You look forward all week to a very special date—and you come down with bronchial morbititus. You're waiting for an important phone call—and you've accidentally left the phone partly off the hook!

A writer must strictly discipline himself in order to accomplish anything. You wouldn't believe how tempted we writers are to roam around the backyard or find any of 1,249 things to do rather than to tackle some sticky writing project! So, a long time ago I decided to glue my nose to the typewriter between nine and one and take time out only for a coffee break.

So much for great intentions! Invariably, someone will call me right when I'm going great on something. Sometimes it will be Mother. "Don't forget my appointment with the doctor at two o'clock, dear," she will remind me. I'll clap my hand to my head. I *had* forgotten—and I had planned to finish a certain writing job that day, and I knew it would take *all* day to do it. With two hours at the doctor's office across town, and getting Mom's prescription, and stopping at the store for bread Mom needed, there went the afternoon!

I don't get the job done that day—but the Lord reminds me that I'm surely blessed to still have my mother around. Frustration may come at the moment—but joy cometh at the thanksgiving.

Then again it might be one of my daughters needing someone to talk to, specifically me. Since they both live in the Atlanta area now and have to call me long distance, I know it's usually important to them when they call on a weekday. But frustrating though it may be to drop work on a project, I do feel gratified that my daughters look to me for a little wisdom, comfort, and prayer. And one of the "hats" the Lord has given me is that of "Mother."

Often a caller during prime writing time has been a

woman seeking counsel and prayer or a hopeful prospective writer seeking advice. Can I let these people down? Can I neglect the writing work that the Lord had given me to do?

In some cases I felt it would be all right to tell the person that I would call them back. One time I did this with a retired teacher who would call me from time to time concerning a letter-to-the-editor I had written that had appeared in the paper. I was working on an important project and wanted to put it in the mail that day.

Even though I explained and spoke tactfully, the lady was insulted and slammed down the phone. Oh, I felt so badly about that, so frustrated! I never wanted to offend that lady, but all she wanted to do was pass the time of day chatting about one of her favorite subjects. That could have waited until after lunch. I still believe I handled that properly.

But then what about those calls from people needing encouragement and counsel right then? I took this matter to the Lord. "Lord, I know You have given me this writing ministry, and You want me to be diligent about it. But I also know that these hurting people are important to You, too."

I just sat quietly for a moment. Then I sensed His message: "Muriel, you take care of My business, and I'll take care of yours."

I understood what He meant. If I helped the hurting ones when they needed me, the Lord would help me get my writing done. It was a fantastic deal—and it has worked ever since I accepted it. So, now when the phone rings during my prime writing time, and it's someone who needs me, I simply leave the writing work in the Lord's hands for the time being and minister to the person.

The automobile provides frustrations, too. It's winter and the hard freeze broke your outside thermometer. You have to drive your children to school. You go out at 7:30, and sure enough the car is covered with ice. You scrape, slip, and slide, and garner your first bruise for the day. Muttering to yourself, you go inside to warm up.

The kids are late getting ready, and you yell, "Come on, come on, kids! You'll be late for school!" Finally you lead them out to the car, step on the starter, and the battery won't turn over. Frustrations!

Life is full of frustrations that we can't do anything about —frustrations that come from people, from inanimate objects, from circumstances. We can become hyper, but where does it get us? Becoming a raving maniac doesn't solve any problems; it just adds to them!

It was frustrating to the apostle Paul to be stoned almost to death, beaten, jeered at, thrown into chains in rat-infested prisons, when all he wanted to do was tell people the good news of Christ.

But Paul turned lemons into lemonade. When he and Silas were beaten and thrown into the Philippian jail, they sat on the dank floor singing praise songs to the Lord at midnight, even though their ministry to the Philippians seemed to have been cut short and their backs were hurting from the metal-tipped lashes that cut them to ribbons.

I've personally found: There is something about singing praise songs that lifts you out of the dankest dungeon of despair and frustration! I think it has much to do with God's pleasure over our faith in Him and our worship of Him during difficult times. He sends His elevating grace.

Anyway, God sent an earthquake that snapped open the bonds on Paul and Silas and threw open their prison doors. He does that for us, too, when we praise Him in the midst of frustrations. He delivers us from our annoyed feelings and gives us a sense of peace about whatever frustration annoyed us.

The Philippian jailer and his family were saved that night; he applied healing salve to the wounds of Paul and Silas;

and the next day the two missionaries were freed to go on with their work for Jesus.

The jailer and his family were possibly among the congregation of the Philippian church when Paul's letter was read aloud. They knew exactly what Paul meant when he wrote, "Rejoice in the Lord alway: and again I say, Rejoice" (4:4, KJV).

9.

Bad Drivers

One time my husband and I were moving from South Carolina to New Jersey. We were pulling a U-Haul with an old green Nash that looked like an inverted bathtub. Suddenly Al found himself driving on a two-lane winding country road behind two old trucks that were going about thirty-five miles an hour. With the trailer on the car, the winding, hilly road, and the occasional cars coming our way, Al found it impossible to pass those two trucks.

"I sure hate to go so slow when we have so many miles ahead of us!" Al exclaimed.

After twenty-five miles of this, the truck in front pulled off. Al heaved a sigh of relief. "Now maybe the guy ahead will go faster!" he said. No such luck! That guy also qualified for the molasses award.

Finally Al saw a clear stretch ahead. He stepped on the gas and started to pass the truck. At that precise moment the driver of the truck turned left without a turn signal! Al swerved the bathtub left, grazing the front of the truck. The bathtub went flying over a deep ditch, and we found ourselves sitting in the middle of a field.

"What'd you think you were doing?" exclaimed the old

farmer indignantly. "Look what you done to my fender! I've a mind to call the cops!"

We weren't going to argue with this man in his home territory, even though he had been in the wrong by not signaling. Al handed him $20, and he went on his way.

"Why don't some people believe in making turn signals?" Al grumbled, as we tried to figure out how to exit that field across the ditch. We finally found a place to do it and went on our way. We both continued discussing bad drivers for awhile.

Then I spotted a happy factor about the whole situation. "Just think, Al," I exclaimed, "if we hadn't had this bathtub, we probably would have turned over when we hit that ditch!" In our thankfulness we dropped the subject of bad drivers.

But bad drivers can really drive you up the pole—or across the ditch or whatever. Take the little-old-lady type. She drives slowly down the middle of the highway, looking neither left nor right. When two cars collide head-on next to her, she exclaims innocently, "Tsk, tsk, why don't those people learn how to drive?" And the dear little instigator of the accident goes on her way without a scratch.

Then there's the drunk who blearily weaves his way down the road. When I see one, I wait until he is momentarily in his lane, then jam the gas pedal to the floor, and get past him as quickly as possible. (Yes, of course, I pray hard and fast!)

Also there is the hotshot weaver who drives like a maniac and weaves in and out of the annoying cars taking up space on the highway. One morning a guy like this was driving to work and wanted to make the yellow light before it turned red. He darted out from behind a car that had stopped and crashed right into the side of my car while my daughter was turning left into her school, thinking the traffic had stopped. That time my car was totaled.

Don't you just love cockeyed parkers? They're the ones who take up two parking spaces with their compact car. Or, if they don't, they park so close to the line next to an empty space that only another small car could fit into the space. Then of course there are the road hogs; the people who think the signal lights on their cars were installed to be used at the exact moment of turning; the jokers who decide to race you when you try to pass them on a two-lane highway; the charming duet who drive down a two-lane highway side by side at forty miles per hour; and the molasses drivers who slowly pull out from a side street in front of you when you're going fifty miles an hour.

Now let's calmly—I said calmly—remember all the people who have dallied when the light turned green and then shot across the intersection just as the yellow light was turning red in our face; and those dear uninformed persons who pile into the right lane and then won't make a right turn on red even though the way is clear!

Let us now have a short moment of silence and also gratitude for all the drivers we have ridden with whose insanity behind the wheel has made us want to get right with the Lord. For those of us who did so at such times when faced with sudden death, it was a blessing, wasn't it?

OK, now for the moment of truth! Let's face it, we have all been guilty of doing something when we've driven that has no doubt delivered devilish diatribes in our direction! I know I have!

So what does Jesus say to us? "He that is without sin . . . first cast a stone." (Or the first nasty look or name or condemnation!)

I suspect that the fruit of the Spirit which most of us have trouble experiencing is patience. Bad drivers can be a blessing to us, brothers and sisters. They can help us to practice patience!

10.
The Wrong Kind of Boss

Before I became a full-time writer, I worked all over the country in all kinds of offices. And I had all kinds of bosses. Some were nice, and some were not so nice!

At several places where I worked I had to keep a desk or something between the bosses and me or somehow intercept the fresh passes they made. I believe that is called harassment. Anyway, I didn't like it! One of these bosses also used to make all kinds of remarks that embarrassed me.

One day a woman from another office, who was working with me temporarily, was incensed by a remark my boss made to me. Since she wasn't under his jurisdiction she had more freedom to speak. And speak she did! "You shouldn't say things like that to this fine Christian lady!" she exclaimed.

I waited until the boss left the room. Then I cheered.

The strangest part about this was that this boss was an ordained pastor of a church, and his head elder was his assistant in that department—and he had groping hands, too! (Or should I say "grubby" to match his mind?) This is another pet peeve: people who profess to be Christians—

especially church leaders—who bring shame on the Lord I love by their low-life behavior!

I worked in another place where the boss was always making seemingly witty, cutting remarks to those under him. One day I came back from lunch and found his lovely, efficient secretary in tears. "I just can't take this much more, Muriel," she sobbed.

I put my arm around her and comforted her. "I understand," I sympathized. "I usually take what the boss says with a grain of salt—but still it hurts!"

Not long after that this secretary transferred to another department. In fact, this man couldn't seem to keep any secretary very long!

Men may not have problems such as women clerical workers have, but they might have a problem with women bosses who are trying to prove their superiority! My daughter worked for awhile as a receptionist for a boss like that, and she suffered from the woman's snappy, insecure personality, as did the men.

Bosses who favor one employee over another are also hard to take (especially when you're not the pet!). Bosses who are supercritical, who have bad tempers, who pay as little as they can get by with are hard to abide, too.

We do have to make a living, though, and good jobs are not always easy to find. The Bible has some wisdom for us in regard to bosses, including difficult ones. First Timothy 2:1-2 tells us to pray for "all those in authority, *that we may live peaceful and quiet lives in all godliness and holiness*" (author's italics). Evidently prayer can help ease our situation when we have a difficult boss!

Paul also told Christian slaves to consider their masters worthy of full respect so that God's name and Christian teaching would not be slandered (1 Tim. 6:1). Even if we find it hard to respect a boss because of what kind of person he is, we can show him respect because of his position of authority.

In his Letter to Titus, Paul instructed Christian servants to be obedient to their masters, to try to please them, and not talk back to them (Titus 2:9).

And Peter told servants to submit themselves to their masters with all respect, "not only to those who are good and considerate, but also to those who are harsh" (1 Pet. 2:18).

The Lord wants His followers to do their best no matter what they do—to "do all to the glory of God" (1 Cor. 10:31). With His help we can, and, in doing our best, it might make the situation easier for us in a less-than-perfect situation.

Dwelling on complaints only hurts us and makes us bitter, resentful, and full of hostility—which, in turn, can wreck our relationships with the Lord and people. Jesus had the right idea when He said, "Love your enemies, . . . pray for them which despitefully use you" (Matt. 5:44, KJV). I've found that this is the way of peace.

11.

Only-Too-Human Co-Workers

This world is filled with all kinds of people, and just as we can't always choose our bosses, so we may have to work with people who bug us.

There's the person who goofs off while we do all the work. Then, when the boss is coming, he makes like he is superworker himself. The boss asks, "How come you guys haven't gotten any further than this?"

Goof-off shrugs his shoulders and remarks casually, glancing at you sidewise, "Well, I can't do it all by myself, can I?"

You react by either angrily defending yourself or clamming up. Then you simmer the rest of the day at Goof-off. That not only deepens your indigestion but also your un-Christian attitude!

Psychologists tell us there are four things which cause us to behave the way we do. They are: (1) stimulus—something comes into our awareness; (2) mental aspect—we accept or reject the stimulus; (3) physiological aspect—our nervous systems react; and (4) resulting action on our part occurs.

It is in the second area—our acceptance or rejection of

the stimulus—where we control the resulting action. For after our nervous systems respond to our mental inclination, we have little or no control. The resulting action takes place.

So the wise thing to do is to learn from your experiences with fellow employees and others—and prepare yourself in case they do something similar again that aggravates you. For instance, in the case of Goof-off, if he pulls that stunt with the boss again, be prepared with a short, intelligent explanation to the boss of what you have done.

Psalm 37 tells us not to fret about what other people do. They may prosper for a while, but they will get their just dues if they haven't done right.

Psalm 37 is a trove of treasures! Commit your way to the Lord, it advises. Trust in him, and He will bring it to pass. Rest in the Lord. Don't fret if someone undeserving prospers for awhile. Cease from anger, and don't lower yourself to do evil as others do. Those who do what is right and trust in the Lord will one day inherit the earth!

When I worked in the shipping office of a printing company as a stenographer and bookkeeper, I would eat my lunch at my desk and read my Bible. One of the men in my office got a kick out of coming up and making fun of me and the Bible, jeering about Adam and Eve, Jonah and the whale, and the like.

I disliked most of what he said, even though I knew he was saying such things to goad me into losing my temper. So, it peeved me.

But as I prayed about the situation, it seemed to me that the Lord wanted me to use this as an opportunity to witness to an insensitive man. So I took each opportunity gratefully after that, and I prayed for my heckling co-worker. Thus the Lord changed an irritating situation into an exhilarating situation.

One time when my husband was pastoring a church in Wisconsin, I worked in a bank as a part-time bookkeeper and stenographer. One of my co-workers, who was a member of a cult, frequently cut me with sniping remarks. I suspect it may have been because I was a minister's wife, for I never said anything unkind to her.

Her sniping irritated me, because it hurt; and I never knew when the sting would bite me. So, as I did with anything that troubled me, I took it to the Lord.

He brought to my attention Jesus' words in Luke 6:27: "Love your enemies, do good to them which hate you"

"All right, Lord, I'll do it," I prayed.

So, after that, whenever the young woman let me have it, I let her have it back in a different way: I found something nice I could say to her or do for her.

I think that came as a surprise to her. Anyway, it wasn't long before she dropped the sniping and became sweet to me.

I wasn't at that place long before my husband took another church in Illinois and I had to leave. Guess who threw the going-away party for me? Uh-huh, the young lady whose sharp tongue had been converted by love!

Understanding and love can work wonders in our relationships with other people. Sometimes when we learn of a person's background, we can understand where he or she is coming from and therefore sympathize with that person. Everyone has problems, and, when they're troubled, they may be difficult to work with. But the Bible says that love covers a multitude of sins (1 Pet. 4:8). And love and prayer can help us bring peace to replace friction!

12.

Fractious Neighbors

Since I grew up in a small country town surrounded by forestry on three sides and was a creative person who marveled in God's creation, I had learned to love nature's natural display of beauty. For a while my family lived in the city, where we had two umbrella trees in front of our house. My father would prune them in the shape of balls. Even at the age of seven, I disliked them. They didn't look natural to me at all. I grew up having little appreciation for foliage as shorn as an army recruit.

So what do you think? Here is this character who loves natural-looking foliage now surrounded on three sides by perfectionists who love strange shapes! I am as out of place as a bum at a high-society tea party!

I have flowers and bushes that bloom in season, growing in profusion all over my property. And I do keep my lawn cut regularly. But one day a neighbor let me know that she and some other neighbors didn't like the way I let my foliage grow. I should cut it all neat and round as she and they did and totally rid myself of flowers she considered weeds. (I'm not talking dandelions here; I do have enough respect for the neighbors only to allow them to grow in my backyard so I can use the leaves for salads.)

I was peeved and hurt. Why couldn't my neighbors let me be me? After all, I tolerated their round shrubs and bushes! But I spoke to another neighbor whom I knew was a mite fussy, and she immediately let me know she didn't like the profusion of flowering plants on my front bank. In her estimation it was an eyesore. "I have to look at that mess from my kitchen window every morning at breakfast, and it annoys me," she declared. (Her lovely home is dressed with three neat round bushes.)

I don't like to peeve my neighbors, for I want to live with them in Christian love. But I didn't want to give up something I thought was gorgeous until I had to. So I decided to compromise.

"I'll tell you what," I proposed. "If you don't mind, I'll continue to enjoy those flowers for this last month of the season. Then I'll get rid of those plants and try to keep a fairly low-profile bank, OK?" And that is what I did. Furthermore, since I knew that some of the foliage along my back fence troubled my neighbors on that side, I removed and killed the offending bushes.

It doesn't hurt to give a bit if it yields peaceful and happy relations with neighbors. After all, the Lord who loves us teaches, "Give to everyone who asks you, and if anyone takes what belongs to you, do not demand it back. Do to others as you would have them do to you" (Luke 6:30-31).

I still can enjoy wildness out in my backyard where the hedge roses, honeysuckle, crown vetch, rose of Sharon, and spirea vanhouttei run free!

Most neighbors fall into the peeve-praise-producing category. One day they'll drive you to muttering, "When's the next flight to Timbuktu?" A few days later they will do something so nice you'll praise the Lord for them.

One man I know drove his neighbor "up the wall" concerning his fence. When he saw the elderly lady had planted some irises next to his fence to keep from losing her soil, he demanded she remove them. "Four inches on your side of the fence is part of my property, you know," he declared in no uncertain terms.

A week later when the neighbor lady had trouble starting her lawn mower, however, he came right over and worked on the mower until he got it started for her.

Let's face it, there are all kinds of people in this world— and in the "it's-just-my-rotten-deal" category, we'll live near someone who has entirely different viewpoints from ours.

If we have children, there's usually at least one bully in the neighborhood. When my older daughter was a child, she got along amiably with just about everyone. But there was one kid who punched her in the stomach shortly after we moved into a new neighborhood. I took it up with his mother, who shrugged her shoulders and didn't see anything wrong with her adorable child slugging anyone!

I became a bit peeved but decided it was her problem, not mine (and I figured it would grow into a real problem someday if she didn't tend to it now!). I just encouraged my daughter to play with other children in the neighborhood. She found a very nice friend—and the day after she received Jesus as Savior, she led her friend to Jesus. The friend began coming to our church with us. So the Lord worked everything for the best.

Yes, I used to get so disturbed when a bully in our neighborhood used to pick on my younger daughter and she would come home crying. I finally had to admit to myself, though, that this dear little girl had a tendency to bring some of that on herself!

And I suspect that many of us bring neighbor trouble on

ourselves! It's not hard. All you have to do is make one peeved remark or stomp on one unguarded foot—and you can erect a spite wall faster than you can say, "Peter Piper picked a peck of pickled problems."

Unfortunately, although Christians are told to forgive one another, we find the same thing happens in churches among Christians—and often it has ended up by splitting the church.

According to Jesus, everyone is a neighbor, and that especially includes our fellow Christians. How careful we need to be that we don't peeve, hurt, or offend our Christian neighbors! I'm afraid more Christians have backslid because they have been peeved by other Christians than for any other reason.

I have found that love, forgiveness, prayer, and returning good for evil is the key to maintaining good relationships with neighbors.

One neighbor I had was a perfectionist. Since she had many problems, I often had the opportunity to comfort her, pray with her, and point her to the Lord. She appreciated having someone she could come to with those burdens, someone who would pray for and with her.

But my two cats annoyed her. Sometimes one of them would walk on her car, and she would see faint footprints. Finally one of them committed the unforgivable sin: he was seen by her boyfriend walking on his car. The friend was furious about it. My neighbor ordered me to keep my two male cats on my own property.

"You can do that with dogs," I protested, "but I don't know how I can do that with these cats who have been used to living outside most of the time. And what about the birds who fly over your car and leave their droppings on it?"

Whoops! I rang the wrong bell with that one! She slammed down the phone. The next day two burly policemen came to my door and warned me to keep my cats on my property, and if they received any further complaints, they would set traps for them and take them away to the pound.

Was I peeved? I was everything having to do with peeved and then some! I was worried about my cats. I tried tying one to a line with a harness, and he got scared to death, scratched me in terror, bolted, and ran away. I sat down in my backyard and cried and cried. "What am I going to do, Lord?" I wailed. After that, I tried to keep the cats in the house as much as possible.

At first I didn't want anything to do with that neighbor. To think that, after all the time I had helped her, she had called the police on me! For several days I avoided her.

But I am used to walking with the Lord, and I knew not only did I have to forgive my neighbor, but be pleasant to her, too, if I wanted to continue walking with the Lord. Also, the Bible says, "Seek peace, and pursue it" (Ps. 34:14). I knew that was the happiest way to live, especially with nearby neighbors!

If I find anything difficult to do in my natural self, I hold it up in my cupped hands and give it to the Lord. Then I find I can do it. So I did this with this neighbor. "I forgive her, Lord. Help me to love her and continue to be friendly and helpful."

He did, and I did. The breach between my neighbor and me was healed, and we went on being friends as if nothing had ever happened. In fact, we went in together to have a nursery tear out the hedge between our driveways and put in flowering evergreen bushes that need little or no care. Then we planted pretty annuals and perennials, and all who passed by admired the new landscaping—a permanent testimony to how love and forgiveness can beautify a neighborhood!

13.

The Belittler and Sniper

Why in the world do some people put down others or make cutting remarks when you least expect them? And doesn't it annoy you to have someone do this to you? Sure, it's natural for us to become outraged when we're belittled or word-speared, because it makes us feel embarrassed or hurt or like something that even the cat wouldn't drag in!

I have known some people who were so belittled by their mates or parents that they developed king-size inferiority complexes. That's sad! For often these are splendid persons who, because of other often less-worthy persons, walk under an emotionally induced cloud that keeps them from realizing their potential as persons. So OK—this is a pet peeve of mine also! I hate to see people mistreated!

As a matter of fact, I'm not too crazy about being mistreated myself. Every time I used to visit with one lady, she would cut me to ribbons with a put-down. Not knowing how to answer her, I'd keep my mouth shut and simmer for a while. The hurt would linger for days; and if what she said referred to something I had done in the past, so would the feeling of guilt.

I went to the Lord about this problem. "Lord, lead me with Your Spirit the next time she does this to me."

He did it! Sure enough, the next time we got together, she let me have it right between the eyeballs. "Help, Lord!" I prayed silently. And help came.

"Well, you know," I replied slowly, "none of us are perfect. We all do things that fall short at times."

She looked at me as if she had run into a brick wall. And she had. I suspect that with that statement I took all the fun out of the put-down for her! After that, she was easier to get along with.

Most of us have been victims of put-downs; some more than others, since they may be married to belittlers or snipers, or have other relatives like that. Belittling and sniping are incompatible with Christ's law of love. So I believe that Christians need to guard against the temptation to put down others. "Be kind and compassionate to one another" Ephesians 4:32 tells Christians.

It might help us to understand why people belittle other people, for understanding increases our ability to forgive. Most belittlers put down others in order to build up their own egos. They belittle to bring someone down to their own level, or they do it hoping to relieve themselves of guilt. For instance, a non-Christian or backslider will belittle someone who is trying to live a good Christian life.

Why do snipers sideswipe us like a hit-and-run driver? People who do this usually have a lot of hostility in them, some of which may even go back to their childhoods. They may have grudges against their parents, other relatives, people who have done them wrong in the past, their husbands, wives, co-workers, or boss.

It often takes very little for them to displace their tamped-down anger and let it out on you in a nasty remark. Jealousy or envy may also net you an undeserved snipe.

One time I went to a ladies' luncheon at a church I attended in California. I was enjoying talking to various ladies around me and enjoying the food. All at once, another young woman whom I barely knew let me have it with a cutting remark. I was stunned!

That happened several years before I committed my life to the Lord, but I decided merely to ignore the woman and continue chatting with the others. Do you know what happened? Before long that young woman was practically standing on her head to engage me in pleasant conversation! I suspect that my reaction to her snipe made her feel a bit guilty and she wanted to make amends.

I learned something from that experience—never to shoot back. And that happens to fit in with Christian ethics. Even though at that time I had no personal commitment to Christ, I had a lifetime of Christian training to guide my response to the sniping sister.

If you have been suffering emotional abuse because of your stand for Christ, the apostle Peter has a word for you:

> Dear friends, do not be surprised at the painful trial you are suffering, as though something strange were happening to you. But rejoice that you participate in the suffering of Christ, so that you may be overjoyed when his glory is revealed. If you are insulted because of the name of Christ, you are blessed, for the Spirit of glory and of God rests on you (1 Pet. 4:12-14).

14.

The Complainer

Complainers are basically negative, unhappy persons. Living with a complainer at home or at work can be like living with an itch you can't scratch. A complainer is always looking for and finding things to grumble or gripe about.

If you're married to a complainer, unfortunately you become specimen #1 for microscopic scrutiny and lengthy discussion, which is otherwise known as nagging. This may happen most often when we try to smoothe the complainer's ruffled spirits concerning other complaints. That's just like standing up in a battlefield with a machine gun aimed at you. Only in this case, the machine gun is a mouth!

Here's what happens: Said complainer puts hands on hips and exclaims indignantly, "You're always standing up for the other person! Why can't you ever see my point of view, for a change?"

Some of us stumble on and make that same mistake of trying to calm the complainer down by mildly pointing out other aspects. You might just as well try to convince a terrorist of the merits of passive resistance. Come to think of it, that simile is halfway good. You end up passive—but I'm not sure about the resistance part!

Proverbs 21:9 says, "It is better to dwell in a corner of the housetop [on the flat oriental roof, exposed to all kinds of weather] than a house shared with a nagging, quarrelsome and faultfinding woman." And Proverbs 27:15 says, "A continual dropping in a very rainy day and a contentious woman are alike" (KJV).

A complaining spirit cannot help but lead to strife. Proverbs doesn't only indict women in this matter but men, too. Proverbs 26:21 says, "As charcoal to embers and as wood to fire, so is a quarrelsome man for kindling strife." Quarrelsomeness often springs out of a complaining, discontented spirit.

At the bottom of most church strife you will often find one or more complainers who spread a dissatisfied spirit among the congregation like a debilitating disease. This is what happened to the children of Israel in the wilderness. God regarded their complaining against Him and His servant Moses as sin, and His wrath and judgment came upon them.

So, when we hear people complaining about other people or situations, we'd be wise not to join them in their discontent. I have found that the best thing to do when something in the church has troubled me—and I can't do anything about it myself—is to pray. In some cases the Lord has answered my prayers; in others He has led me to move on. I don't think in any case, however, does He call on us to aid in the destruction of a church and its testimony in the community! And that is often what complaining to others does. That's why it peeves me when I hear one Christian tearing another apart! (That's complaining, too.)

There's nothing much we can do to change complainers. The desire to change must come from within the persons themselves. They must finally realize how destructive their negative way of looking at life is. It's possible for this to happen.

I know one young woman who had always been a negative-thinking complainer, a difficult person to live with. When she came into daily contact with another such person, she finally realized what a miserable, foolish way of life that was. Then she made a concerted effort to change into a positive-type, unpicky person. It has done wonders for her personality and relationships!

I prayed a lot for this young woman, so perhaps the Lord opened her eyes in answer to my prayers. Anyway, it certainly is worth a try, for the Lord is the great Eye-opener!

Paul told the Ephesians, "I pray . . . that the eyes of your heart may be enlightened in order that you may know the hope to which he [God] has called you, the riches of his glorious inheritance in the saints, and his incomparably great power for us who believe" (Eph. 1:18-19). Believe me, if people have the eyes of their hearts enlightened like that, they'll quit complaining instead and start glorifying the Lord with thanksgiving. There's no room in a thankful, praise-filled heart for griping!

Perhaps you have been aware of a tendency to complain about things. One time I suddenly realized I had caught the complaining spirit and was talking negatively about others. I knew the Holy Spirit was convicting me, and I felt so ashamed! Falling on my knees in repentance, I asked the Lord's forgiveness and help in controlling my mind and tongue in this area. And you know, the Lord is so gracious! He does help us overcome our failings when we repent and seek His help!

God answers prayers for others—and for ourselves!

15.

The Gossip

"I think we really need to pray for Marie and Bert," someone will say confidentially.

"Some special reason?" you ask curiously.

"Oh, didn't you hear? Marie found out Bert was cheating on her with the blonde in the second row of the choir, and they got into a big fight, and Bert has moved out!" The words tumble out like a blurb for a prime-time soap opera.

Now if you're like most people, you'll stay eagerly tuned in for the gory details. But when we learn that people are gossiping about us, WHOOM! We get peeved to the gizzards! Then we're not impressed by the fact that Gracie Gossip prefaced what she said by asking prayer from us. We suddenly see that as simply an excuse to pass along juicy tidbits of tantalizing tattle.

When the shoe is on the wrong foot—ours—we feel it like a new-grown corn. But when it's kicking somebody else, I suspect we can hardly wait to get to the phone to pass it on to others with embellishments!

Just like complaining, gossip is an old habit with mankind. Proverbs 18:8 says, "The words of a talebearer are as wounds, and they go down into the innermost parts of the belly."

Matthew Henry wrote, "Talebearers are those who secretly carry stories from house to house, which perhaps have some truth in them, but are secrets not fit to be told, or are basely misrepresented." According to him, they blast people's reputations, break friendships, make mischief between relations and neighbors, and set people at variance.

God's Word says, "Whoever slanders his neighbor in secret, him will I put to silence; whoever has haughty eyes and a proud heart, him will I not endure" (Ps. 101:5). God's Word makes no mistakes. When it puts things together, they usually go together!

I played a game called "Gossip" at a party one time. The first person told a story to the next, and so on. After it made the rounds, you'd hardly recognize the story it was so embroidered. That's how gossip works, and for that reason it peeves me. It also peeves me because of all the harm it does to people and churches!

Somebody may see the pastor standing outside a beer joint with a "painted lady." He may be waiting for the woman's half-drunk husband, so he can drive him home and witness to him—but by the time the story runs full circle, the poor preacher was supposedly reeling from drunkenness and having an affair with the lady!

When I realized the harm that gossip can do to people and the Lord's work, I was convicted about having done my share. After all, nobody likes a good story as much as a writer—and nobody can embellish it so well as a creative person! (Maybe some career gossips would make good novel writers.) Anyway, I went to the Lord and told him how sorry I was for gossiping and asked His forgiveness. Since then, I've found the Lord has given me the power to resist the urge to pass along juicy junk.

Proverbs 26:20 says, "Where no wood is, there the fire goeth out; so where there is no talebearer, the strife ceaseth." If you want to squash burgeoning dissension in your church, put a clamp on the gossip!

I've also found that I've felt uncomfortable at times with someone whose mouth I can't trust. Proverbs 20:19 says, "A gossip betrays a confidence; so avoid a man who talks too much."

Unless gossips are convicted about their hurtful habit, there's not much we can do about them except pray. But for ourselves, let's take to heart what Psalm 15:1-3 says:

> Lord, who may dwell in your sanctuary? . . . He whose walk is blameless and who does what is righteous, who speaks the truth from his heart and has no slander on his tongue, who does his neighbor no wrong and casts no slur on his fellow man.

16.

The Exploder

There goes Mount Vesuvius again, blowing his top, the hot lava falling on you. You retreat literally or mentally, more than annoyed that once again a microscopic spark has set off the fireworks. I say "blowing *his* top," because men more often resort to this defense or offense than women do. Women are more apt to deal with things by clamming up, so we'll use "she" in that chapter more often. But there are volcanoes and clams in both sexes.

We most often resent being dumped on when we feel we're the scapegoat; and the most common scapegoat is the spouse. A guy comes home after a rough day at work, and he's ticked off about something the boss said. Only he couldn't answer the boss back. So what does he do? He simmers and stews until he comes home.

As he walks in the door, his unsuspecting wife asks, "Honey, did you pick up some bread for supper, as I asked you this morning?"

Ka-pow! The whole hostility falls on her hapless head! *Wha'd I do?* she wonders. *What'd I do?*

Or suppose a husband is an amiable guy, and his wife goes firecrackers easily. He comes home from work tired,

wanting to sit down and watch the evening news. His wife
has had a difficult day, and she has burned the chicken. As
her husband settles comfortably in front of the TV, she
marches in, and the tirade falls on this "beast" who has the
nerve to relax when she can't. *Wha'd I do?* he asks in confu-
sion. *Wha'd I do?*

What these two poor dumped-on ones did was marry
someone who probably has built up hostility since child-
hood—or, if not that, they have acquired since then the
ruinous habit of brooding and holding grudges. If a psy-
chologist gave them the standard test for attitudes, they'd
probably blow the top of the hostility score!

If it's any comfort to you who are married to exploders,
it's probably not so much you they have hostile feelings
toward as themselves or others. Exploders may have an
inferiority complex caused by their experiences in life with
others, which results in their resenting anyone who in the
least way threatens the little self-esteem they may have for
themselves.

God's Word does not excuse an angry person, however.
In fact, it warns, "Do not make friends with a hot-tempered
man, do not associate with one easily angered, or you may
learn his ways and get yourself ensnared" (Prov. 22:24-25).
This is reason enough for us to avoid hostile people when
at all possible.

If you're married to such a person, that's hard to do. But
I know one woman who took refuge in working outside the
home and being active in her church. She particularly found
a more peaceful life when she worked a different shift than
her husband. (She didn't believe in divorce, and she wanted
to save the marriage, if at all possible.)

The Bible also gives us some recipes that will help us if
we have to live or work with a hostile person. Proverbs
15:1 says, "A gentle answer turns away wrath, but a harsh

word stirs up anger." I have learned from personal experience with angry people that this works!

Proverbs 17:14 advises, "Starting a quarrel is like breaching a dam; so drop the matter before a dispute breaks out." (Just don't drop it on Exploder's foot!)

Let's admit it—most of us have exploded at one time or another and have peeved others. Our children sometimes have the ability to elicit this response. Or we may become infuriated with a neighbor, relative, co-worker, or acquaintance and let fly with the mouth.

With God's help we can control the temptation to fly off the handle by deciding how we will handle it before any trying event comes up. Ecclesiastes 7:9 says, "Do not be quickly provoked in your spirit, for anger resides in the lap of fools."

We can also control our future actions by ridding ourselves of hostile thoughts and attitudes, by forgiving *everyone* who has ever hurt or offended us. This clears the way for love to control our words and actions.

Ephesians 4:26-27, 29-32 is a super minimessage on getting victory:

> In your anger do not sin. Do not let the sun go down while you are still angry, and do not give the devil a foothold. Do not let any unwholesome talk come out of your mouths, but only what is helpful for building others up according to their needs, that it may benefit those who listen. And do not grieve the Holy Spirit of God. . . . Get rid of all bitterness, rage and anger, brawling and slander, along with every form of malice. Be kind and compassionate to one another, forgiving each other, just as in Christ God forgave you.

17.
Me and the Dumb Things
I Do

Have you ever said or done something so dumb that you would kick yourself—if you weren't afraid of putting your sacroiliac out of whack? (No sense in compounding dumbness!) In this chapter the pet peeve is *ME!* I think one of the dumbest (and one of the most expensive) things I ever did was trying out my daughter's new skateboard (which in my vocabulary is now another word for *disaster*). We had gone to celebrate Christmas with my brother and his family in Florida. When I went to put the gifts we had received in my car trunk, I got this brilliant idea: *Why not test ride this skateboard on Gene's driveway? It's smooth and has an incline. And I've always liked to skate.*

So here is this lady in her forties heading blithely down the drive on a skateboard. And here is this skateboard hitting a small patch of sand at end of said driveway. And wham! Here's the dignified matron being slam-dunked face first onto the asphalt street!

See said matron slowly rise, picking up her broken glasses and holding her front-tooth crown in place, and staggering into the house.

Brother runs up and exclaims, "Oh, Sis, you're bleeding —you've hurt yourself!" (Excellent observation!)

"Please push my tooth crown up in place if you can!" dumb lady lisps, and Brother carefully does what he can.

After he washes blood off dum-dum's face and sits her in a chair to recover from shock, he takes her glasses out of her clutching hand and says he'll see what he can do about putting the frames back together.

Total cost of ten-foot skateboard ride: Over $700 for removal of broken tooth and three-tooth bridge-crown combination installation and new glasses.

Then there are the ordinary dumb things we do from day to day. Did you ever go to introduce somebody you've known for five years to somebody else—and have the name slip into the deep recesses of your mind? You hem and haw and finally end up saying half apologetically, "I want you to meet a friend of mine."

Speaking of memory work, I have often sung with my accordion at rest homes, missions, and prisons, setting my music on a stand in front of me. One time I went to a rest home with a group, and I knew these people usually did everything perfect, by heart. So I chose a song I had sung many times before and felt I could play and sing it without words and music in front of me.

I failed to take into account my "Blanko" factor. Halfway through I forgot some words in the second verse. There is something about doing such that wipes you out almost completely! Sure, I stumbled on and did the best I could—but I couldn't live with myself for two days after that! (I've never sung in public since then without my music in front of me. It's a wise person who knows his own shortcomings!)

Have you ever played a chess game, and you're moving along nicely with your own plan to check the other person's king—and all at once your opponent shouts, "Checkmate"?

Or a checker game, and before you know it your opponent is going JUMP, JUMP, JUMP, JUMP—"Heh, heh, sorry about that!"

Have you ever taken a wrong turn—and ended up in a tough section of town? Have you ever made an appointment and forgotten to keep it? Have you ever run into somebody who greets you like an old friend and you can't remember where or when you knew this person or who they are?

Like many ordinary people, I've been doing dumb things all my life. When I was three, I banged my head on the pavement because I was jealous of my new baby brother and the attention he received. (Hey, maybe I can use this to account for doing other dumb things?)

When I was eight, I accidentally kicked some sand at a kid when I arose from a park sandpile—and got beaten up by a horde of his brothers, sisters, cousins, and second cousins who considered it a personal affront. (Since some of them pounded me on my head, this gives me another excuse for future dumbness, right?) But no matter how many excuses I can find for doing dumb things, I still feel bad about myself when I do them.

When I was fourteen, I entered an amateur contest at my high school. My piano teacher had never emphasized my memorizing what I played in public, so, when I went to play a solo on the piano, I had my sheet music in front of me. A spotlight glared at me. As I went to quickly turn the page while playing, the light caught me right in the eye and, fumbling with the page, I dropped it on the floor!

Deep silence while Muriel Koller, sophomore, reached down to the floor to pick up her page. After what seemed like three hours (it was only thirty seconds, but you know how it is!), Muriel finally put the page in place and continued on with flaming red face (which looks colorful with her blond hair).

To add to the entertainment for the day, following Muriel's personal disaster came another girl playing a violin solo. She played one piece—while the pianist played another. She joined Muriel in the red-face department, and that day the two "les miserables" became buddies. Afterward the music teacher lectured each girl privately, letting them know what idiots they had made of themselves. They really didn't need to be told—they knew it already!

At the time I made that embarrassing mistake, I was really upset with myself. But I'm thankful now for that boo-boo, because it gave me a best friend for the rest of my high school days. And I'm thankful, too, for other mistakes I have made, because I have learned important lessons from them. I'm even thankful for the accident that forced me to buy an upper bridge of three crowns, for they made me look so much better when I smile.

When I was in high school, something else happened that annoyed me about myself. I wanted to be an artist because I seemed to have a talent in drawing. But my talent was strictly in sketching figures—and the art teacher preferred teaching painting, charcoal work, and designing. While my other marks were mostly in the nineties, I was given a consistent 83 in art. After two years I finally became discouraged and switched to a commercial course—typing, stenography, and bookkeeping.

Now that I look back, I can see God's hand in this, as well as in so many others things that happened to me. God wanted me to become a writer for His glory, and those commercial skills I learned and the subsequent office jobs I held were to prove among the finest preparations for being a writer. (At Christian writers conferences I have taught a course called "The Business End of Writing.")

Thus I have seen that "all things work together for good to them that love God, to them who are the called according to his purpose" (Rom. 8:28, KJV). How wonderfully comforting that truth has been to me as I have gone through life!

Through realizing my fallibility, I have also realized my need to depend completely on my all-powerful Lord. I may fail—but Jesus never fails! I have also been filled with awe at His love and patience with a person of clay such as I. I appreciate Romans 5:8 which says, "But God commendeth his love toward us, in that, while we were yet sinners, Christ died for us" (KJV).

I don't think the Lord wants us to go on kicking ourselves for dumb things we do or have done in the past. We can learn from them, but we usually can't undo them. The Bible teaches that when we repent and trust in the Lord, He forgives us and removes our sins "as far as the east is from the west" (Ps. 103:12, KJV).

Jesus teaches us to forgive all those who offend or hurt us, and I believe that includes forgiving ourselves. Jesus wants us to be His lights—and how can we be if we are busy brooding over dumb things we have done? For fretting is self-centered and keeps us from sharing our love with others. Brooding keeps us from being filled with Christ's peace and joy that radiate like sunbeams from Christians who have them.

No, sir! Out with the self-peeves and in with the Lord's peace—and joy and love!

18.

The Steamroller

The Milquetoasts of this world are the victims of the steamrollers. I used to be numbered among the Milquetoasts and was periodically used or flattened!

I came to realize, however, that even though Christians are to be humble and cooperative, they also are accountable to God to use their time wisely, to do what He wants them to do, and to stand up for what is right and biblical. So just as the Holy Spirit has given me power to witness for the Lord, He has also given me power to say "no" and to take whatever stand He desires for me. The Holy Spirit has given backbone to this jellyfish!

Webster defines the colloquial meaning of steamroller as "any agency that ruthlessly overrides and crushes." And we have folks in this world who do that to other folks.

Parents do it to their grown children; grown children do it to their parents; bosses do it to their employees. Christians do it to other Christians. Various strong-willed family members always get their own way while the rest stew. When you have two steamrollers in a family, the contest of wills is exhausting to the rest of the family. Steamrollers are not

in the habit of listening to other people. Things must always
be done their way. They are right, period.

How in the world can a person reason or live with a
steamroller? It's pretty hard, unless you're willing to give
in at every point. I don't think it's Milquetoast to give in or
compromise with a steamroller whenever feasible. As
Christians we are to seek peace and pursue it. But if a
steamroller wants me to use my valuable time to do something, and I know God wants me to use it to write or do
something for Him—God wins every time! I am pleasant
but firm.

Steamrollers in churches ride all over the Milquetoasts,
who mutter to themselves and to others about programs
and ideas that have been instituted that perhaps the majority
are not happy with. So they become peeved. One reason
some are troubled is because they happen to be in the path
of the steamroller and they are run over and crushed.
Steamrollers usually don't mean to hurt anyone, but in
order to obtain their goals, they have to. This ends up being
painful to the victims.

Do you know what happens in the church when this
situation occurs? People drop out rather than become involved in power struggles. The Holy Spirit is quenched too.
I was once active in a church where this happened. I saw a
church where I had once felt the presence of the Holy Spirit
become like a dead, dull shell of what it had been. I, as well
as others, no longer felt the presence of the Lord, and it
made me feel so sad.

I have seen this happen when some full-of-wonderful-
ideas new young pastor has come into a church. He will
immediately see things that must be changed right away,
and enthusiastically he'll set his mind to implement his
plans. But the Old Guard will dogmatically protest, "We've
never done things that way before!" So the steamrollers

meet head-on—and the sheep (an apt designation Jesus gave His followers) become divided or scattered.

Our Lord doesn't want His people to be steamrollers. Through the apostle Paul God said, "If you have any encouragement from being united with Christ, if any comfort from his love, if any fellowship with the Spirit, if any tenderness and compassion, then make my joy complete by being like-minded, having the same love, being one in spirit and purpose. Do nothing out of selfish ambition or vain conceit, but in humility consider others better than yourself. Each of you should look not only to your own interests, but also to the interests of others" (Phil. 2:1-4).

This means being willing to give and take. If you have good ideas, you share them; and if the rest of your brothers and sisters think they're worthwhile, then you can go ahead as a family and initiate them. Often we accomplish at least some of the goals we have by talking things over and working things out through prayer. But if we have to stomp on a brother or sister to do it, Jesus won't like it!

Philippians 2:5-8 admonishes us, "Your attitude should be the same as that of Christ Jesus: Who, being in very nature God, did not consider equality with God something to be grasped, but made himself nothing, taking the very nature of a servant, being made in human likeness. And being found in appearance as a man, he humbled himself and became obedient to death—even death on a cross!"

Humility helps us overcome steamroller tendencies. So does *agape* love. It seems as if the closer I draw to the Lord, the harder it is for me to hurt anyone else. It's as if I am hurting my own self; and according to Jesus, we are doing to Him what we do to any brother or sister (see Matt. 25:34-45).

Although God is not willing that any should perish, God does not force us to accept Him, for He wants us to turn from our evil ways and come to Him in response to His love, as revealed through His dying on the cross for our sins. If God, who is all-powerful, does not resort to steam-roller tactics to enforce His desires, who in the world are we to steamroll for our own desires and aims, however good they may be?

The Bible teaches that God is love, and He wants His followers to be love, too. "Love is patient, love is kind. . . . It is not rude, it is not self-seeking, it is not easily angered. . . . It always protects, always trusts, always hopes, always perseveres. Love never fails" (1 Cor. 13:4-8).

19.

Car Repairs

The peeve of feeling gyped for car repairs is so widespread that every so often you see an exposé article in some publication. A reporter will take a car that has been thoroughly checked over by a good mechanic to various garages for repair estimates. He comes up with quite a good story: most of the garages proposed to do work that was totally unnecessary!

I've had a lot of experience in this department. One time I noticed that the front tires on my car were wearing unevenly. *Looks as if I need a front-end alignment,* I muttered to myself.

Scanning the newspapers ads, I spotted a sale price on alignment. (Take it from me—responding to a sale on anything having to do with car care is like inviting a shill to run the store!) Anyway, I took my car to garage A. After shopping for an hour, I returned.

"Sorry, lady," the mechanic exclaimed, "I can't do an alignment on your front wheels—your ball joints are shot! Take a look!"

My car was on a lift, and the mechanic wiggled its right-front wheel. "See?" he said. "It shouldn't go like that. You definitely need new ball joints." After giving me a price, he said he could do the work right away.

I told him I'd think about it (because I remembered a recent experience my father had had at this garage.) After being horrified by all one garage had estimated needed to be done to his car, he had taken it to this place, where the list of repairs was entirely different.

What's a person to do? I sighed. *I don't know if this mechanic is telling me the truth or not!* My car was quite old, and I had begun to suspect I'd have to replace it. So I didn't want to put any more money into it than necessary.

A brilliant idea hit me as I headed for home. I decided to take the car to another garage and just have them switch the front tires. That way they'd wear on the other side. After garage B switched my tires, they told me my car needed new lower bushings.

Now I was really puzzled. Why had one mechanic noticed I needed new ball joints and this other one, new bushings? "I'll think about it," I answered.

Eight months went by while I thought about it. In the meantime my front tires had become bald on one side.

Checking the ads, I noticed that garage B had a sale on both tires and alignment. So I drove to garage B.

"The last time I was here," I explained to the manager, "I was told my car might need new lower bushings." After mentioning the price quoted, I asked him to install them also.

When I returned, the manager had bad news for me. "We didn't do the alignment, ma'am, because we wanted to check with you first about the bushings. It wasn't the lower bushings that were bad—it was the upper bushings, and they cost three times as much. We can't do the alignment until they're replaced."

I shook my head. Now I was really confused! I asked

about the tires. He suggested I get them replaced by their branch store across town where I had bought them. "They're probably covered with a guarantee, and you can get an allowance on your new tires there."

Thoroughly confused by all the different diagnoses, I stopped by garage C to have the car checked and get their price on bushings.

After checking, the mechanic declared, "The bushings are all OK, ma'am!" So I drove across town to get my new tires and an alignment.

After shopping for a while, I returned to find my two new tires had been mounted—but the wheels couldn't be aligned until *my ball joints* were replaced!

I asked him the cost, and it was higher than garage A had quoted. "You also need a brake job," the manager reported. "We have a sale on brakes right now, and we can do brakes and ball joints right now if you'd like."

"I'll have to think about it," I answered, bewildered.

Who can I trust? I murmured in frustration. *Who can I trust?*

I drove back to garage C and asked the man to check my car again, telling him of the new diagnosis. After inspecting the car, he advised, "Your ball joints are OK, but your left tie rod needs replacing—and you do need new brakes."

I asked him the cost, and he quoted it to me. "I'll think about it," I answered once more. This was becoming a stock phrase with me—I was in a rut in more ways than one in the car repair department.

I was so annoyed, because it was all so confusing that I didn't know what to do or who to believe!

Shortly after this my teenage daughter solved the problem. That was when she had made the left turn to her school on a yellow light, and the speed demon had crashed into the front end of old "Betsy." Talk about "out of alignment," you should have seen the front end of that car! Lori was OK, but Betsy was totaled.

Oh, well, I needed a new car anyway. Betsy was beginning to burn oil. The Lord replaced Betsy with a "cream puff" of an LTD-2 Ford that was the same color Betsy was, and was quite a bit younger!

I've thought about how we let ourselves become all upset about mundane things, and then we wonder why we develop hypertension. The lady we rented our house from years ago told me her husband had died of a heart attack when he saw how some tree cutters had butchered his favorite tree.

Having our cars repaired, and many other things to take care of, can indeed be trying. But I take everything to the Lord and seek His wisdom. For instance, since "Betsy" was totaled, I have found a Christian repairman I feel I can trust. He not only fixes my car, but does my plumbing and electrical work, too.

We can be thankful if we have a car to take us places. It's better than having to walk or having to take care of horses and hitch them up or take a stagecoach! Thankfulness can banish our chagrin and fears and give us a new perspective on problems.

One of my favorite Scriptures is Proverbs 3:5-6: "Trust in the Lord with all thine heart; and lean not unto thine own understanding. In all thy ways acknowledge him, and he shall direct thy paths" (KJV).

The Lord knew Betsy was going to be totaled. Look at all the car repair money He saved me with the confusing diagnoses!

20.

The Judge

Have you ever had someone look down his/her self-righteous nose at you because you did something they didn't approve of? It's annoying, isn't it—especially if you don't see anything wrong with doing that particular thing and you think it's a man-made legalism.

I suspect that some Christians have a lip-smacking, satisfying time in life making themselves feel as if they are better than anybody else by judging others. I also suspect that some of these "goodies" never stop to wonder if they do this because in their hearts they feel they aren't what they should be with the Lord. (Oops! There I go a-judging!)

If it's any comfort to you, even the holy God Himself was judged and criticized when He walked the earth. The Carp boys of Jesus' day (AKA Pharisees) tore Jesus apart for eating and drinking with sinners such as tax collectors and harlots. They jeeringly called Him a "winebibber."

They found fault with Jesus for not making His disciples ceremonially wash their hands before they ate, and for allowing them to pick some grain to eat on the sabbath. Then they hypocritically questioned him about the legality of His healing a man's shriveled hand on the sabbath (see Matt.

11). After He had the nerve to do that right before their nearsighted eyes, they went out and plotted how they might kill Jesus! (When men start talking about killing the Son of God, there has got to be something wrong with their hearts, no matter how righteous they appear outwardly!)

Jesus looked on their hearts—and what He saw turned His stomach.

> "Woe to you," He cried, "teachers of the law and Pharisees, you hypocrites! You shut the kingdom of heaven in men's faces. You yourselves do not enter, nor will you let those enter who are trying to. You blind guides! You strain out a gnat but swallow a camel. You snakes! You brood of vipers! How will you escape being condemned to hell?" (Matt. 23:13-14,24,33).

Both sides of the coin concerning judging our brothers and sisters and our doing something that might cause them to stumble are dealt with by Paul in Romans 14:13: "Therefore let us stop passing judgment on one another. Instead, make up your mind not to put any stumbling block or obstacle in your brother's way."

People at the church we joined in New Jersey years ago thought mixed bathing was OK, but going to movies was a sin. (I grew up in a seashore resort, so I always thought swimming was OK.) But when my husband attended a Bible college in Columbia, South Carolina, we soon learned that mixed bathing was considered a sin in parts of the South—but going to movies was OK, as long as you didn't do it on Sunday!

Later, when my husband pastored a small country church in Wisconsin, we found that the people did not approve of women using lipstick, wearing earrings, or having short hair. I knew that as the pastor's wife, I especially should respect their beliefs concerning holiness. Out of love for them and consideration for my testimony before them, I put aside my lipstick and earrings and let my hair grow long.

It didn't cost me anything to do that (what I lost in artificial beauty aids, I gained by having long blond hair—especially when people looked at the back of my head), and it certainly helped keep peace in the church.

At the next church my husband pastored, in Illinois, we found that the ladies enjoyed wearing lipstick and earrings and wore all lengths of hair. So I dug my lipstick and earrings out of the bottom drawer and added them to my long blond hair. Now my looks were not so bad on the front side. One important item I should mention here is that my husband's opinion was that any old barn looked better with a coat of paint!

Seriously now, the Lord Jesus Christ did tell His followers,

> Do not judge, or you too will be judged. For in the same way you judge others, you will be judged, and with the measure you use, it will be measured to you. Why do you look at the speck of sawdust in your brother's eye and pay no attention to the plank in your own eye? (Matt. 7:1-3).

None of us are perfect, and only God knows our hearts. Romans 14:10—recorded by the apostle Paul, whose inspired letters told Christians how to live—says, "But you, why do you judge your brother? Or you again, why do you regard your brother with contempt? For we shall all stand before the judgment seat of God" (NASB).

Getting those North, South, and Midwest Christian viewpoints was good for me. What effect did they have on me? Most importantly, I learned to depend on the Holy Spirit and God's Word as my guide to right and wrong. I saw along the way that the same legalism the Pharisees lived by sometimes exists among us Christians. I wanted to live a life pleasing to my Lord under grace, not law. This is not to be a life of license but of holy love.

I also learned to refrain from judging other Christians if their beliefs concerning Christian living differed from mine —even if I felt that certain Scriptures taught that something they were doing was wrong for Christians. They are responsible to the Lord, not me! I was just to love them.

If some of my brothers or sisters in Christ are doing something I feel might hinder them or others in their Christian walk, then I pray for them. If what they're doing is sin by scriptural standards, I ask the Lord to grant them repentance that they might come to their senses and escape from the trap of the devil. (See 2 Tim. 2:24-26).

In this passage of Scripture Paul told Timothy to instruct gently such people (not harangue, not lecture, not gossip about, but gently instruct). So, if I have a burden of concern on my heart for someone I think is in Satan's trap, I pray for the Lord to lead me about how to speak with them when a good opportunity should arise. Such opportunities do come about when those I'm concerned for seek my counsel or we have friendly conversations.

I see Christians all around me whose lives or marriages have been hurt or ruined by the roaring lion. Let's not judge them—let's pray for them!

21.

Le Phone

You have to leave in two minutes. You've been trying to get through to someone on the phone for the past hour. It's vital! It's urgent! Shriek! You have just become Type A.

Beep . . . beep . . . beep—again that impersonal sound which has the amazing potential of turning a perfectly normal person into a blithering idiot, pounding his head on the wall if the circumstances seem to call for it. I sometimes wonder if we'd have less trouble with high blood pressure if Alexander Graham Bell hadn't had such a brainstorm!

The phone is a profound blessing, but I suspect that it also is one of our greatest frustrations. Did you ever call a business and have them put you on hold—and you listen to some kind of music for several minutes before you realize they have forgotten you?

Sometimes they do return after two or three minutes. I am a busy person and hate to lose that time, so I have put a neck rest on my phone. Before I make such a call I lay out work on my desk. Then I don't mind waiting.

Here are three of the main phone peeves, all illustrated in the same scintillating story: You undress, step into the shower, for which you have finally gotten the hot and cold

water adjusted, get soaking wet from head to toe, and then
. . . *ring, ring, ring.* Did you ever notice that nobody seems
to call before you step in, nobody seems to call after you get
dried and dressed—it's always at the precise moment when
you're soaking wet, and *especially* after you have applied
shampoo to your hair, and there is no one home but you!

So, on the first ring you leap out of the shower, grab a
towel as you're going down, and wrap it around you en
route to the phone. You reach the phone and find one of
two things: either the person hangs up precisely as you pick
the torture tool up, or an excited voice exclaims, "Congratulations! You have just won one of three exciting prizes
—a gold Cadillac, a trip to Hawaii for two, or a genuine
zircon ring.!" Guess which one it will turn out to be?

"What's the catch?" you mumble.

"No catch," supersalesperson answers pleasantly. "All
you have to do to claim your prize is to drive to Oceanview
Acres and pick it up."

"Where's that?"

"Just drive 275 miles northeast from Greenville to Po-
dunk; turn right at the swamp after you pass Mosquitoville
Haven, and you'll see our sign in a mile or so. After our
representative shows you our captivating condominiums
with an ocean view, he will give you your prize!"

"No, thanks," you mumble, dropping the phone. You
head back for the shower, tracking more water on the floor,
suddenly in a concrete-chomping mood.

Have you ever called someone and had a toddler answer
—and give you baby talk for two minutes? That's cute, but
so often the child hangs up on you. Have you ever been
awakened out of a sound sleep and a fascinating dream, and
had someone ask, "Is Jake there?" (How insulting! What
would Jake be doing in my apartment at three in the morning?) Have you ever had a stranger dial your number acci-

dentally, and you skid up to the phone and answer—and the cockeyed dialer asks, "Who is this?"

And here is a pet peeve that women and girls especially have: obscene phone calls. You answer the phone all innocent and unsuspecting—and here comes this remark that makes your ears curl and your face turn three shades of red. When this first happens, you scream, "What did you just say?" (you don't really want to know); or you slam down the phone. With those reactions you have given the pervert some satisfaction.

Now that you know how vile the real world is, the next time this happens you restrain yourself, hang up the phone, and call the police. Usually they don't do anything until the calls have become obnoxiously repeated.

Sometimes a person you may know starts doing this to you. After I had received three such calls in row, I suspected this might be the case. *How can I make this low-life stop?* I wondered.

Then it occurred to me that even this could be used as an opportunity to witness. Not only that, but a short sentence about Jesus Christ could really turn such a caller off, so that he might never call again. It would spoil his fun completely.

So I asked the Lord what I should say if I should receive another dirty call. He laid on my heart a short sentence. The next time I got an obscene call I hit the guy right in the ear with: "Did you know that Jesus Christ died for your sins?" I think he was "shook up" then! He hung up immediately.

That brief answer I believe God gave me can do several things. It can convict the man of his sinfulness and tell him of the remedy.

Afterwards I prayed for that man's soul, that the Holy Spirit would convict him and speak to his heart through my sentence. Only the Lord can help a sin-sick soul!

So we can use "le phone" as an opportunity to speak for the Lord, not only to obnoxious callers, but to Christians and non-Christians alike who may call us. The Bible says, "But sanctify the Lord God in your hearts, and be ready always to give an answer to every man" (1 Pet. 3:15, KJV).

I know that verse goes on to say more than that, but in conjunction with other verses in God's Word, I believe it applies. Let's be ready "in season and out of season" to use every opportunity we can to witness and point others to our Lord. If we accept the phone as another instrument to serve the Lord, we can rejoice in its invention!

22.

The Debater

We all know at least one arguer. I'll also call him or her a debater. That's the person who will turn the most trivial comment or conversation into a king-size argument. Sometimes I think such people must lie awake at night trying to think up various opinions that might differ minutely from any idea anyone might mention to them.

"Nice day today," you comment innocently.

"Yeah, but I think it's going to rain."

"Why, there's not a cloud in the sky!" you answer. "And the weather man gave only a one percent chance of rain for today."

"There, y'see! Just like I told ya—it's going to rain!"

"Wasn't that a great sermon the pastor preached on Sunday morning?" you remark, changing the subject.

"Uh, huh—if you like taking your nap between eleven and twelve in the morning!"

"Well, I appreciated the way he encouraged us all to witness for the Lord," you reply blandly.

Congratulations! You have just opened the door for Debater's favorite subject. "What's the point of witnessing?" Arguer snaps. "Don't you know that all those of us who are elected to be saved will be saved?"

You've been through this before, and you don't want to go through another two hours of fruitless debate about biblical doctrine. You snap your trap shut and excuse yourself for whatever reason you can honestly use.

Proverbs 17:14 observes, "Starting a quarrel is like breaching a dam; so drop the matter before a dispute breaks out."

I suspect a lot of marital problems are increased by argument. One word leads to another, and the repartee becomes worse and worse. It may advance even to gross name-calling, accusations, and physical attacks.

If both persons involved in a disagreement are contentious people, that's *big* trouble! But if only one of the two is like that, there is some hope. Proverbs 15:18 says, "A wrathful man stirreth up strife: but he that is slow to anger appeaseth strife" (KJV). So here is a clue to those of you who have to deal with contentious persons. Seek the Lord's wisdom in dealing with such persons to mollify them.

I know one man who has been contentious most of his life. Would you believe that his grandson has accidentally stumbled on a way to turn him from his contentious spirit? Whenever this man begins complaining about someone, and he's ready to argue at the drop of a pinkie, his grandson —who finds him hilariously funny when he does this— laughs and exclaims, "Oh, Grandpa, you are so funny!" Then the grandfather laughs, and the two start exchanging light repartee.

I'm not sure a husband or wife could get away with this, but we can pray about how to calm down whatever contentious persons we may have to confront. The best way is simply not to argue. It takes two persons to make an argument.

Sure, we may disagree. But is it worth getting into an unpleasant tangle? Proverbs 26:3 counsels, "Do not answer a fool according to his folly, or you will be like him yourself."

Because a debater likes to argue, we may not get very far by reciprocating with such a person. But sometimes we can plant ideas—through literature we leave around, through turning on radio or television programs, or through relating an interesting story about someone who is doing something we'd like to get across. Eventually if the arguer thinks it is his own idea, he'll end up doing what you've felt was sensible all along. Yes, it takes patience—but it's more fun than an argument!

23.

The Clam

There are at least three species of human "clams." There's the person who uses clam power as a reciprocal weapon with a mate (or coworker or friend) who tends to be an exploder or arguer. There's the person who has been hurt by somebody else and doesn't want to talk to that person. And there's the person who doesn't want to discuss marital or other problems.

The "silent treatment" can be very effective in troubling another person. For this reason it is not a method the Lord would usually condone (although He used it effectively when He was falsely arrested, accused, and brought to trial).

In the context of marriage, clams may have various reasons for not wanting to discuss problems with their mates. They won't talk things out, and they usually won't go to a marriage counselor with their mates, either. Why not? Well, they may always end up on the short end of an argument, especially if married to an exploder or arguer. Or they may prefer talking to friends instead of talking to their mates. They may be hiding something, or they may be natural clams.

A husband and wife can't put important differences on a back burner—where they'll simmer, burn the pot of marriage, and finally explode into separation or divorce. That is exactly why so many marriages are ending in divorce. For one reason or another, many couples just won't or can't talk out their differences. This factor may be one good reason for people who separate, putting off getting a divorce.

I know one couple who couldn't seem to communicate with each other and finally separated. But during the weeks that followed they realized they really loved and missed each other. They started seeing each other—and suddenly found it possible to discuss the differences they had in their marriage. Thus, they were reconciled.

Jesus gave His followers a principle to follow when there were differences between them. "Therefore," he declared in His Sermon on the Mount, "if you are offering your gift at the altar and there remember that your brother has something against you, leave your gift there in front of the altar. First go and be reconciled to your brother; then come and offer your gift" (Matt. 5:23-24).

The following words He spoke may well be applied to married couples in particular today: "Settle matters quickly with your adversary who is taking you to court. Do it while you are still with him on the way, or he may hand you over to the judge . . . and you may be thrown into prison. I tell you the truth, you will not get out until you have paid the last penny" (vv. 25-26). Many a person has experienced the essential truth of this!

If there is a "clam" who has been causing you distress, perhaps you can ease the problem by examining your particular situation. Sometimes we never stop to check what we're doing to warrant a "clam" response; it's easier to blame the other person!

Do you tend to have a bit of the "exploder" or "arguer"

in your nature? Through the power of the Holy Spirit you can have victory over these tendencies. For when we are filled with the Spirit, we manifest His fruit, which includes love, gentleness, patience, and humility. The Spirit becomes the ruling influence in our lives rather than the flesh.

The apostle Paul realized how "flesh" control messes up a person's life and makes it miserable. He discussed this in detail in Romans 7, where the subject was "I, I, I" (which often gives rise to the exclamation with the same phonetics). He ended by exclaiming, "What a wretched man I am! Who will rescue me from this body of death? Thanks be to God—through Jesus Christ our Lord!" (vv. 24-25).

He didn't stop there, though. He went on to Romans 8, where the subject is living in the Spirit. Compare how often the Spirit is mentioned in this chapter with how often "I" is used in chapter 7! Romans 8 explains how Christians are rescued from control of their fleshly leanings. It works—it really does!

And one last word to clams: As long as you play "clam," it indicates that you are holding something against the person to whom you are not speaking. God's Word says to you,

> Therefore, as God's chosen people, holy and dearly loved, clothe yourselves with compassion, kindness, humility, gentleness and patience. Bear with each other and forgive whatever grievances you may have against one another. Forgive as the Lord forgave you. And over all these virtues put on love, which binds them all together in perfect unity (Col. 3:12-14).

24.

Slovenly Christians

Speaking as a person who really cares about God's work being done properly, one of my biggest pet peeves is the slovenly service many Christians give their heavenly Master! I am usually a pretty easygoing person, but this really upsets me! And I suspect that other conscientious Christians in positions of church leadership also get upset over this widespread situation.

Perhaps it is because I worked in the business world for so many years. I saw that employees were expected to do their jobs and be dependable. If they didn't, they were laid off. So, most employees from the top to the bottom did their work conscientiously. Security and money provided strong motivation.

I have also held positions of leadership (teacher or director in some phase of Christian education) in churches across the nation. So, I have been greatly frustrated at times by the way some have let God's work down! In all fairness I must say I've known a number of faithful Christians, too, who have been a joy to my heart.

At one church I served as the superintendent of the Children's Sunday School assembly, and each Sunday led the large group of Primaries and Juniors (that's what we called them then) in a short opening exercise.

At that time my younger daughter was in the Primary 2 class. I noticed that the teacher, who was the Sunday School superintendent's wife, came only once or twice a month. I also learned that the superintendent would stand by the front church door at 10 AM, when we started and nab whoever he could to go teach my daughter's class at the last minute. Among those he would send down were twelve-year-old girls and folks who hadn't come to church for a month!

The superintendent knew better than that, for I had heard him instruct the teachers in a Sunday School meeting to call their substitute if they couldn't come in, preferably the night before.

I was concerned. I wanted my daughter and the other second graders to learn something from their class and to have a caring teacher! I spoke to the superintendent, and he replied, "Well, when my wife works the night shift, she sometimes doesn't feel like coming in on Sunday morning."

I was chicken—I didn't have the nerve to suggest she give up the class to someone else. But I spoke to the pastor about the situation, thinking he could take up the matter with the superintendent. He just shrugged his shoulders, though, and answered, "Well, the twelve-year-olds have to learn how to teach sometime, don't they? It's good experience!"

"Without any preparation or training?" I gasped.

"Oh, they probably do all right. Don't worry about it!" But this was *God's* work—and I was concerned. Can you imagine what would happen if a business were run like that? And this concerned little children.

Since there seemed no more I could do, I decided all I could do was pray about the problem. Eventually the Sunday School superintendent's wife gave up the class, and someone more regular took it over. By that time, however, my daughter was in Primary 3, which had a good, dependable teacher.

Remember that the King's business is *our* business, if we are His followers! How can we take it so casually? How can we not care about the way it is conducted? For the way we do God's work affects other people.

God's Word tells Christians, "Let all things be done decently and in order" (1 Cor. 14:40 KJV).

If Christians agree to teach, I feel it should be with the commitment of making sure their class has a prepared teacher, either studying the lesson beforehand themselves, or letting a substitute teacher or superintendent know in time so that another qualified, prepared teacher might take over. If Christians accept positions of authority, they should learn how best to do the job and do it conscientiously, just as they would if they were appointed superintendent at a plant! They should be dependable at all times.

Every Christian is given at least one gift with which to serve in the church. Jesus doesn't want them to wrap it in a napkin and bury it in the ground; He expects them to use it for the benefit of His other children and for His work.

From what I have heard from various church leaders, however, the majority of ablebodied Christians don't want to be bothered doing anything for the Lord. They want to be free to live their lives for themselves. Will Jesus call many of these someday, "Thou wicked and slothful servant"? He may also say concerning these, "And cast ye the unprofitable servant into outer darkness: there shall be weeping and gnashing of teeth" (Matt. 25:26, 30, KJV).

I suspect that most professing Christians today do not rightly fear the Lord. They call Him "Father," think of Him as a friend in need, and sing "Amazing Grace." But they do not fear the omnipotent, Holy God who is supposed to be their Lord and Master and who will hold them accountable one day for how they obeyed Him and did His work on earth. Psalm 2:11 says, "Serve the Lord with fear, and rejoice with trembling" (KJV).

As you can see from my rhetoric, this business of slovenly servants of God is a genuine 100 percent pet peeve of mine, and I don't find humor in it. That is because it hurts me so to see our loving Lord and His work treated in such a shabby fashion! How can we really love Him and not give Him our very best?

Colossians 3:23 challenges, "Whatever you do, work at it with all your heart, as working for the Lord, not for men, since you know that you will receive an inheritance from the Lord as a reward."

25.

The "Establishment"

Let's hear it from all those who have ever had a pet peeve against the "establishment," the government! I suspect nearly 100 percent of us participate in this peeve. Consider all the peeve possibilities here: taxes; red tape; taxes; postal service; taxes; pork barrels; taxes; boondoggles; taxes; fiscal irresponsibility; taxes; corruption; taxes; oppressive or immoral laws, etc., etc., etc.

OK—let's take taxes. When I finally finish preparing my income tax forms, including the horrendous job of "self-employment" math, I have this diabolical urge to write "Infernal Revenue Service" on the check. I fight it with all my strength—then limply write the proper name.

Have you ever noticed that the "Ides of April" occurs inexorably at least once a year? (OK, fellow Latin students, I know I'm using "Ides" loosely here—but the day of dread used to be on the real Ides in March!) If I were a scientist, I'd like to do a correlation on the incidence of this Ides with attacks of nervous problems, ulcers, and apoplexy, not to mention drunkenness, family abuse, and marital breakups!

I suspect the Government seeks out the most-educated bureaucrat to obfuscate the forms we bewildered taxpayers must fill out. A new "easy" form to provide more accurate information for payroll deductions was sent to every taxpayer early in 1987, and it serves as a prime example. The government had to recall it and issue a different one because nobody could understand the first, and the entire nation had been reduced to blithering idiocy from frustration!

In Washington, Congress blithely votes for billions in spending projects, many of which are pork barrel stuff. The same goes on in state capitals. We taxpayers get the bill and end up working for the Government until May before the money we make is ours!

There are federal taxes, state taxes, county and city property taxes, sales taxes, hidden taxes. But when they start messing us up by taxing yard sales, they'd better watch out! Going to yard sales is one of my favorite hobbies, and when I heard the local tax raisers were toying with this idea, I was about to become a flaming radical crusader! I know all yard sale addicts can relate to me on this. And who can live on a free-lance writer's income without yard-sale bargains? Would you believe I even bought my travel trailer at a yard sale?

Tax collectors were a pet peeve in Jesus' day, too. The Jewish leaders had a fit when they saw Jesus actually associating with those fellows. But Jesus came to call sinners to repentance. God the Son loved the tax-collectors, harlots, lepers, and other outcasts of society so much that He died to save them and give them everlasting life. Sure, He died for the Pharisees, too; but most of them were too proud to accept Him.

The Pharisees wanted to trip up Jesus and get Him in trouble with the people. So knowing how unpopular the Roman tax was with the people, they asked Jesus, "Is it right to pay taxes to Caesar or not?"

Jesus sensed their evil intent. "You hypocrites, why are you trying to trap me?" he exclaimed. "Show me the coin used for paying the tax." So they did.

"Whose portrait is this?" He asked, pointing to the coin. "And whose inscription?"

"Caesar's," they answered.

"Give to Caesar what is Caesar's, and to God what is God's," Jesus answered (Matt. 22:17-21).

And Jesus Himself, when asked to pay the tax, sent Peter to catch a fish, which had in its mouth a coin that paid both His and Peter's taxes.

Thus the Lord set the example and supplied the need. If we're making the money that results in the taxes, why don't we relax and quit fretting over the taxes we must pay? For if we belong to the Lord, He has promised to supply all our needs!

Please don't get me wrong! I love my country and think it's the best in the world—and I pay my taxes faithfully. (Take it from me—a self-employed person has literally a four-times harder task at that, too!) I also acknowledge that there are many fine, faithful people serving our government, including those in the IRS. But, like all good loyal Americans, I complain a little, too.

Most business and professional people and farmers may have red tape, and the accompanying 429 simplified forms, to fill out at the top of their peeve list. Part of their problem may be their own fault. They should have foreseen the sticky mess of red tape and taken three years extra training at a university graduate school on how to fill in the papers and still have time for their work. Please don't ask me which university has this vital course—I don't know.

But you can ask me about red tape, inefficiency, and the government's waste of taxpayers' money. I ought to know. I worked for the U. S. Government at Fort Monmouth,

New Jersey; Lakehurst Naval Air Station; and the Tennessee Valley Authority. To be fair off the top, I'll have to state that many government workers are efficient and dependable; I had to score high marks on a variety of tests in order to land my positions. And many departments are run very well indeed. But this is a book about pet peeves, so I'm pouncing on them.

When I started to work at Fort Monmouth, I was assigned to the Purchase Department, along with fifteen other people who needed to brush up on Perry Mason.

"What does Perry Mason have to do with it?" you may ask with raised eyebrows. Well, for three months we had nothing to do except pass around and read the Perry Mason paperbacks the messenger boy brought in. Hold it—I take that back! I did log in the workers' attendance every morning.

After three months the department was dismantled, and we were reassigned to other departments. I served as a stenographer and also filled out forms and delivered them in my new department. One form required eight copies, but I never did find out where the second pink copy was supposed to go—so I just hid it in with our file copy (smart thinking, eh?).

Now, I'll not say any more about red tape, waste, and inefficiency. I'm sure many of you could write reams about it. Come to think of it—why don't you do it and rid your system of the frustration?

And now for the post office. I know it's now supposed to be run privately—but the Government still has a lot to do with it, because it is the only monopoly the Government will permit.

I've sent a letter to my daughter in the next state—and she has received it in one week. I've sent something here in town, and it's made it to the other side of town in three days. I've received mail from clear across the country in two days from the postmark. You figure it out. I believe there may be hope for better local delivery, though.

I must stop here and commend all the faithful, hardworking postal employees, many of whom endure all kinds of nasty weather and scurrilous attacks from barking biters, bitter boors, and bee swarms in order to deliver our mail to us. My mother was the postmistress of our town and had to work six days a week, twelve hours a day for pittance wages; and, though she was faithful and did her job well, she absorbed plenty of flack. And my brother was a postal clerk in the Navy.

As a writer, I am intricately involved with the postal system, so naturally it is one of my favorite pet peeves. Since I started writing in 1960 first-class postage has been sextupled—but payment rates from Christian publications have only been doubled or tripled, at most.

Hey, all you struggling free-lance writers out there! The starting postal worker now is paid $22,500 a year, far more than most secretaries, and out of sight as far as our income is concerned. Why not take a job as a postal worker—retire in twenty years and write to your heart's content?

I won't be gross and go into gory detail about the condition mail is delivered in sometimes. Suffice it to mention that I've received some looking as if it had gone through a train wreck caused by a Guatemalan earthquake—and then had an oil truck explode in its vicinity.

And why should I mention junk mail? I must restrain myself here. Let's just say that if I laid all the advertisements and appeals for money end to end, they would reach clear to Outer Mongolia. And may all those junk mailers who print on the front of the envelope dire threats like "Urgent —Open immediately—Federal Offense etc., etc." be ashamed of scaring old folks to death!

Seriously now, dear friends and countrymen, let's not complain about the Government unless we are willing as citizens to do all we are free to do about it! We have the privilege of voting out incompetent and uncaring officials and voting in responsible, caring men and women who will support most of what we believe in. The majority of the world is under Communist or despotic domination, and the people do not have that privilege. Nor do they have the blessed privilege we have of freedom to worship our Lord and tell others about Him. Let's count our blessings—and we have many here in America.

Paul wrote in 1 Timothy, "I urge, then, first of all, that requests, prayers, intercession and thanksgiving be made for everyone—for kings and all those in authority, that we may live peaceful and quiet lives in all godliness and holiness. This is good and pleases God our Savior, who wants all men to be saved and to come to a knowledge of the truth" (2:1-4).

Our prayers for those in authority can help them to have wisdom and to do God's will and can contribute to our own happiness and freedom to worship and witness. This, in turn, can result in many coming to our Lord Jesus Christ for salvation, love, joy, and peace!

26.

The Smoker

You've heard the classic, "Smoke Gets in Your Eyes"? Well, when it comes to having a smoker in your vicinity, it's more like "Smoke Gets in Your Eyes (nose, hair, clothing, *and* lungs!).

Have you ever noticed (if you're not a smoker) how the smoke will drift lazily through the air from someone's cigarette (or cigar or pipe)—and will zero in on your nose? That is uncanny! I have thought that smoke had a directional signal hidden somewhere in its haze!

I never started smoking for three reasons. My mother didn't smoke, and I looked up to her as what a good mother should be like. When I was seventeen my boyfriend handed his cigarette to me and told me to take a deep drag on it—and I almost hacked myself to death.

When I was eighteen and working as a secretary at Lakehurst Naval Air Station, I'd go into the women's small restroom, and all the other gals would be puffing up a storm. One day one girl asked me, "You don't smoke, do you?" (Brilliant observation!)

I shook my head in a *no.* "Well, don't ever start!" she exclaimed emphatically. "I wish I never had—but now I can't stop!'' That declaration was better for me than any preacher's sermon.

Even though I have never smoked, I don't look down on those who do. In fact, I have deep sympathy for them, for most developed the habit when they were too young to realize what they were getting into. Just about everybody smoked when I was a young woman; it was "the thing to do."

My older daughter, Gay, says that one of her biggest pet peeves is to go into an expensive restaurant—and—just as she and her family are about to eat a high-priced dinner—the people at the next table start smoking up a storm and, of course, as mentioned before, the smoke always zeros in on nonsmokers! "It robs me completely of all appetite," Gay complained to me. "It isn't fair!''

When my husband was attending Bible college, I worked in my landlord's "Nifty Sweet Shoppe." At times you could cut the smoke in there with a Samurai sword! I'd go home with my clothes and coat stinking like a carton of burned cigs.

We attended a church where it was taught that cigarettes defiled the body, which is the temple of the Holy Spirit (1 Cor. 6:19-20). Me and my stinking coat would go to prayer meeting and put half the people into a state of shock. So, you see, you can't judge a schnook by its cover!

Years ago people laughingly called cigarettes "coffin nails.'' Since then scientific research has proven they were aptly named, since they have killed thousands through lung cancer and heart attacks. Even though my beloved father gave up smoking a year after he received Christ as Savior at the age of fifty-one, he developed lung cancer in his seventies and died from it.

Doctors have discovered that sometimes the effects of

carcinogens show up twenty or thirty years afterward. Nevertheless, I'm sure that giving up smoking adds years to the lives of many. I rejoice that my father was able to serve the Lord and witness for Him for twenty-seven years.

Smokers not only condemn themselves to an early grave, but they condemn loved ones and others. According to the American Public Health Association, tobacco fumes from co-workers are killing 3,200 nonsmokers a year. In 1987 this organization asked the government to order an emergency ban on smoking in all indoor workplaces. They claim this would effectively eliminate nearly 67 percent of the lung cancers that nonsmokers contract from inhaling tobacco fumes in the air. Thus, a heavy smoker violates God's Commandment, "Thou shalt not kill."

From interviewing Christians who had once been slaves to alcohol, I've learned that they found smoking harder to give up than booze! Nevertheless, any born-again Christian smokers can do it, with God's help. And since they are Christ's representatives on earth and their bodies are the temples of the Holy Spirit, they would be wise to give up cigarettes or any other defiling or enslaving habit. Then others would really see Jesus in them!

My father, brother, and husband were all chain-smokers when they came to Jesus; and through His help and power they were all able to give up cigarettes.

And you cigar and pipe smokers can also prolong your lives and the lives of others. That also goes for those who dip and chew "smokeless tobacco." Statistics concerning the harm of smoke and smokeless tobacco are staggering.

Come out from under the smokestack, brothers and sisters, and serve Jesus as a clean vessel! God's Word promises, "No temptation has seized you except what is common to man. And God is faithful; he will not let you be tempted beyond what you can bear. But when you are tempted, he will also provide a way out so that you can stand up under it'' (1 Cor. 10:13). If you will stop making excuses for using tobacco, you will have the victory!

27.

Family

No matter how wonderful one's family is, there is probably at least one member who does or says things that annoy us. In fact, maybe everyone in the family has at least one quirk that quivers us. No matter how patient and cheerful we usually are, there are times some family member peeves us. I'm usually a reasonably cheerful and fairly patient person myself, but I have to admit that this is true of me!

I suspect, for instance, that no matter how old children may become, their parents—their mother especially—may tend to speak to them as if they were still ten years old. I love my mother dearly, but I must admit that this tendency on her part sometimes sets my time bomb a-ticking!

"There's a stop sign ahead!" she'll exclaim, jamming her feet on the car floor. "You'd better stop." (I have stopped for stop signs since I earned my driver's license when I was seventeen.)

"Mom," I'll come back tightly, "why do you always tell me how to drive, when you've never had a driver's license —and I've been driving practically all my life?"

"I just don't want you to make a mistake," she'll answer, rather subdued.

Short silence. "Did you forget you're taking me to the doctor's office—we're not going to church now?" Mom reminds. "Shouldn't you have gone straight a while back?"

"Oh, no," I groan. "I just automatically went this way. I wish you had said something sooner!"

"Well, I know you don't like me to tell you how to drive."

And then there's the other direction in the generation gap, where you're the parent and the kids drive you looney. There's something to be said for kids who dawdle or constantly squabble with one another, or come in looking like they've gone on safari through Mud Jungle. If it's any comfort, consider the fact that they'll be paid back when they have kids! Ditto for teenagers!

Then, of course, there are brothers and sisters, in-laws and outlaws, infighting and outright fighting, and power politics. The truth is, as long as we have individuals of different basic personalities in the family, we will sometimes be downright frustrated with each other.

My two daughters, Gay and Lori, provide good illustrations here. Gay is basically a gung-ho, sanguine-choleric type, and, as such, has succeeded as a top award-winning real estate salesperson in the Atlanta area. She's personable, outgoing, strong-willed, independent, optimistic, and confident.

My younger daughter, Lori, is as different from Gay as a person could be. She is predominantly of a melancholy temperament, sensitive, impractical at times, doesn't make friends as easily as Gay does, and is talented in art to the point of genius. She has won twelve national and area awards for her art and has sold some of her writings.

Both of my girls were top honor students in school, but with all their brilliance of intellect, they simply don't understand each other! And at times they are frustrated with each other because of this. There is quite a span between their ages, which also may have a bearing on their relationship. This accounts, too, for the reason that one generation may not understand an older or younger generation.

I tell my daughters this: "The closer we draw to the Lord, the closer we draw to each other, and the more understanding and patience we'll have for each other. Jesus fills our hearts with His love when He is first in our lives. And love covers a multitude of sins—and misunderstandings!"

I believe this biblical truth not only applies to families related by the flesh, but also to the family of God. As I have walked with the Lord, a tremendous love has grown in my heart for my Christian brothers and sisters—those who love and know the Lord and seek to follow and serve Him, regardless of their denomination or Christian fellowship, or what personality type they may have. This, in turn, has helped me to have more understanding and patience with them.

In every fellowship we have all types of people. We have the "old guard," which usually resists change, and the younger set which comes in with new ideas. We have creative, sensitive people who are offended at the drop of a feather—if they're not asked to sing, if they're not mentioned in the bulletin, or if they're moved from the front row of the choir to the second row! We have other impulsive types who don't stop to think how their ideas, actions, or words might hurt someone else.

We have many "babes in Christ," such as those in the church at Corinth. The Lord has balanced the church by having more mature types like Paul to teach and encourage the babes in the way they should go.

In families related in the flesh, the immature members usually cause rifts or schisms; and this is true in the church.

"What? Are you saying Deacon Loggerhead is immature? Why, he's at least fifty years old, and he's been saved for thirty years!"

Let's face it, natural and spiritual maturity have nothing to do with years! Some Christians, like Paul, may be only three years old spiritually and yet more mature than most of the longtime Christians in the church. That is because they have grown in grace and knowledge of the Lord through walking with Him, obeying Him, and delving into His Word.

The apostle Paul, by inspiration of the Holy Spirit, told the Colossians, "So then, just as you received Christ Jesus as Lord, continue to live in him, rooted and built up in him, strengthened in the faith as you were taught, and overflowing with thankfulness" (2:6-7).

The apostle Peter wrote to Christians,

> So get rid of your feelings of hatred. Don't just pretend to be good! Be done with dishonesty and jealousy and talking about others behind their backs. . . . cry for this, as a baby cries for his milk (1 Pet. 2:1-3, TLB).

Whether we're three months or forty years old in the Lord, we still can begin maturing in Him by following the God-given advice shared with Christians by these two stalwarts of the faith.

Let's love one another enough so we won't become disgruntled! For we are one in the Lord. Just consider the exciting calling Peter tells us we have:

> But you are a chosen people, a royal priesthood, a holy nation, a people belonging to God, that you may declare the praises of him who called you out of darkness into his wonderful light. Once you were not a people, but now you are the people of God (1 Pet. 2:9-10).

28.

What to Do with Your Pet Peeves

Ever since Adam and Eve sinned in the Garden of Eden, bringing woes on themselves and their posterity, mankind's life has been filled with all kinds of troubling thistles and thorns. God gave the first man and woman a perfect environment and they were happy in their innocence. But they flunked the test of obedience to God—and we've been flunking it ever since!

We'll have to admit it—because of our inborn sinful nature and the fact that none of us are perfect, we all do or say things at times that may peeve someone else. That's the old fallen human nature popping up. And we all will encounter situations and people who will peeve us.

Jesus recognized our situation in this tarnished world of ours when He said to His followers, "These things I have spoken unto you, that in *me* ye might have peace. In the world ye shall have tribulation; but be of good cheer; I have overcome the world" (John 16:33, KJV). Through our Master we too can overcome the vicissitudes of life. Here are some biblical suggestions about how we can do this through Him.

(1) *Go to the Lord*—Some things peeve us because they

cause us anxiety or worry. The psalmist exclaimed, "I sought the Lord, and he heard me, and delivered me from all my fears" (Ps. 34:4, KJV). This is one of my favorite Scriptures; in fact, the whole chapter has meant so much to me that I memorized it. Whenever anxiety starts troubling me, I quote this verse to myself and look up.

I awoke in the middle of one night not long ago with an anxious feeling. As I quoted the verse, I seemed to go into some kind of trance. Looking up, I saw Jesus looking down at me. He extended His hand toward me, and I saw the letters G-R-A-C-E come down and touch me. The anxiety disappeared. Thus I believe the Lord let me know through a vision that His grace will dispel all fear whenever we look to Him.

(2) *Rest in the Lord*—So often we Christians will bring the things that are troubling us to the Lord—and rise from our knees with the burden still on our backs.

One time I found a friend deeply troubled about her younger son, because he wasn't doing well in school. She was a little peeved about the situation. "Have you taken all this to the Lord?" I asked.

"Oh, yes, of course."

"If you left it with Him, you wouldn't still be troubled," I pointed out. "Let's kneel down together, and pray, and you give it all over to the Lord."

We did that and my friend found peace.

Not long after that the Lord led the parents to put this manually inclined lad in a vocational school, where he found his place. He is now a splendid Christian man with a good Christian family.

Psalm 37:7, 9 touches on this subject relating to peeves with other people: "Rest in the Lord and wait patiently for him; fret not thyself because of him who prospereth in his way, because of the man who bringeth wicked devices to pass. For evildoers shall be cut off, but those that wait upon the Lord, they shall inherit the earth" (KJV).

3. *Trust in the Lord*—The daily problems of life—finances, frustrations, lack of cooperation from other people—may indeed peeve us, thus robbing us of peace.

In regard to daily needs, Jesus said, "Therefore, I tell you, do not worry about your life, what you will eat or drink; or about your body, what you will wear" (Matt. 6:25). Then He pointed out how, if God feeds the birds and clothes the lilies of the field in splendor, will He not much more care for His own people?

"But seek ye first the kingdom of God, and his righteousness," Jesus taught, "and all these things shall be added unto you" (v. 33, KJV).

Regarding daily frustrations, why not claim for yourself Psalm 62:8? "Trust in him at all times, ye people; pour out your heart before him: God is a refuge for us" (KJV).

What does it mean when God is our refuge? It means that we need no longer stew over the daily peeve producers. Our emotions need no longer be stirred up in ways that are harmful to us physically, mentally, and spiritually. David sang, "I have set the Lord always before me; because he is at my right hand, I shall not be moved" (Ps. 16:8, KJV).

4. *Believe in the Lord*—Some of you who have read this book may be peeved because one church says this about the way of salvation and another church says that—and you don't know what to believe. Why not just believe what the Bible says?

Romans 3:23 says "all have sinned." After reading this book on peeves, we sure know that! Romans 6:23 says "the wages of sin is death; but the gift of God is eternal life through Jesus Christ our Lord." Salvation is a gift from God—accept it! Also know that God never goes back on His Word. Romans 5:8 says that God demonstrated His love for us, "in that, while we were yet sinners, Christ died for us." He loved *you* so much that He died for *you!* Look up. See Him suffering and bleeding on the cross for your sins. (All verses in this paragraph are KJV.)

Romans 10:9 says if we confess with our mouths the Lord Jesus, and believe in our hearts that God has raised Him from the dead, we will be saved. And Romans 10:13 declares, "Whosoever shall call upon the name of the Lord shall be saved" (KJV).

If you have never realized that Jesus Christ died on the cross for your sins, if you have never repented of your sins and received Christ as your Savior, why don't you settle your salvation right now and give your heart to the Lord? I did that one day some years ago while sitting at my desk in an office. And that day Christ transformed my life and gave me a new purpose. That day faith also moved in, and my doubts were resolved.

John 1:12 says, "But as many as received him [Jesus Christ], to them gave he power to become the sons of God, even to them that believe on his name" (KJV). (See also John 3:16 and Acts 16:31.)

When you receive Jesus Christ as your Savior, He comes to dwell in you through the Holy Spirit, who causes you to be born into God's family. The Holy Spirit will also enlighten your understanding and guide you into all truth. (See John 16:13.) Then you will understand God's way of salvation more fully. God's Word will become a new book to you; you'll love reading it!

5. *Live for the Lord*—When we truly follow the Lord and seek to obey His will as revealed in His Word, peevishness will not rob us of peace and joy.

When people are often peevish, it's because they are thinking only of themselves, and not of the Lord and others. We have some older saints in our church who suffer various ailments and could be peevish about them—but everytime I see them I thrill at the light from heaven that makes their countenances glow!

Chronic peevishness is a way of darkness. But Jesus Christ said, "I am the light of the world; he that followeth me shall not walk in darkness, but shall have the light of life" (John 8:12, KJV).

6. *Rejoice in the Lord*—Have you ever noticed how so many of the psalms started out by complaining to the Lord? But the complaining spirit was banished when those psalms started praising and thanking the Lord for His goodness, His mercy, His grace, His dependability, His care, and His love!

Whenever I find myself feeling peevish about something, I say to myself, *Here, now, I am not going to give up the peace and joy of the Lord because of this!* At such times I may not feel like praising and thanking the Lord—but I start doing it anyway. I just think of all I have to be thankful for and rejoice in the Lord for those things. Wow! That peevish spirit disappears and I find myself waxing enthusiastic in my rejoicing in the Lord. Why not try this the next time you're feeling peevish? It works!

Romans 8:18 says, "For I reckon that the sufferings of this present time are not worthy to be compared with the glory which shall be revealed in us" (KJV). In this passage of Scripture we see that all of creation groans in pain because of the bondage of corruption, and we also groan within ourselves awaiting the redemption of our bodies.

When Jesus Christ returns to earth again, that wonderful thing will happen! First Corinthians 15:52 says we'll be raised from the dead with incorruptible bodies. The old fleshly, self-centered self will be gone, for we shall be like Jesus! Peeves will be a thing of the past.

For the Lord himself will come down from heaven, with a loud command, with the voice of the archangel and with the trumpet call of God, and the dead in Christ will rise first. After that, we who are still alive and are left will be caught up with them in the clouds to meet the Lord in the air. And so we will be with the Lord forever. Therefore encourage each other with these words (1 Thess. 4:16-18).

See you there!